Enjoy the walks, and may the sun shine all
day, your boots feel comfortable on your feet
and your pack feels as light as a feather!
Happy walking!
John N. Merrill

Something to ponder.

As we walk around this amazing world, we take for granted the stunning diversity of life and nature. We pass the slopes of mountains and the river valleys. We see birds, insects, animals and all the kaleidoscope of flowers and trees. But let's stop for a moment and just stand in awe of this plethora of sights. However hard we, as humans try, we cannot match the magnificence that our eyes see. Whether you are spiritual or not, you cannot ignore or be moved to wonder at the incredible work of a higher dimension - the divine.

While many would say this is evolution, there still has be "someone", who first thought up the flower, tree, bird, animal, and landscape. You only have to gaze at a small mountain flower and see the delicate stems and petals made to perfection. Whilst the earth's movement have created our landscape, the forces of the divine have been at work to help create that breathtaking view. We on the other-hand have been given eyes and feelings, so that we can appreciate and stand in awe at the sight before us.

So as we wander down a path in woodland or high mountains, where the whole spectrum of life is laid out for us to see. Lets give eternal thanks for being able to walk and see these things first hand. To be able to touch, feel and appreciate the work of the divine, makes the effort more than worthwhile. So, as you walk, stop and ponder at the never ending variety of sights and smells that confront us on each stride we take.

John N. Merrill 2014

WHY I WALK *by Revd. John N. Merrill*

I walk for the exercise; to stretch my legs and muscles; to suck in the fresh air and be free in the wide, wide world, as I walk upon Mother Earth.

I walk to see the trees; that sway in the breeze. To watch the leaves flutter in summer and to walk through on the ground in November. I observe the quietness of winter and watch the buds form ready to emerge when it is their time.

I walk to see the wild flowers; the wood anemones, the blue bells, red campion, and orchids that grow in Spring and early summer.

I walk to listen to the birds that sing in the hedgerows and trees. The friendly Robin is not far away, the started Jay or motionless heron standing at the waters edge. A sudden flash of blue as a kingfisher shoots by.

I walk to see the wild animals; the red fox, the deer, the squirrel and the insects and butterflies, like the dragonfly and red admiral butterfly.

I walk to see the views; to ascend a lofty peak and sit upon the summit surveying everything below, like an eagle high in the air.

I walk for solitude; peace and quiet, to go back to the basics of life, where it is just man and the elements.

I walk in the sunshine, the rain, snow and wind. All has its own beauty and characteristic. All are the cycles of life. I admire the cloudless sky and the rolling clouds of wind and storm.

I walk to see the work of man and God, knowing that we are all connected. Everything has its own beauty.

As the sun sets and I walk home, I know I have lived and experienced a full day, witnessing the whole spectrum of life. I am grateful, very grateful, that God gave me two fine legs, a healthy heart and good lungs to see paradise on Earth.

© Revd. John N. Merrill 2012

HOW TO DO A WALK

The walks in this book follow public right of ways, be it a footpath, bridleway, Boat or Rupp. which are marked on the Ordnance Survey 1:25,000 Explorer Series of maps.

On each walk I have detailed which map are needed and I would urge you to carry and use a map. As I walk I always have the map out on the section I am walking, constantly checking that I am walking the right way. Also when coming to any road or path junction, I can check on the map to ensure I take the right route.

Most paths are signed and waymarked with coloured arrows - yellow for footpaths; blue for bridleways - but I would at best describe them as intermittent. They act as confirmation of the right of way you are walking and the arrow usually point in the direction of travel.

The countryside has the added problem of vandalism and you will find path logo's and Information Boards spray painted over and even path signs pointing the wrong way! That is why I always advise carrying the map open on the area you are walking to check you are walking the right way. In my walking instructions I have given the name and number of each main and minor road, canal lock and bridge number, together with house numbers where you turn and the name of the inns passed. Wherever I add what the footpath sign says, plus the stiles, footbridges and kissing gates en route. All to help you have a smooth and trouble free walk.

I confirm that I have walked every route and written what I found at the time of walking.

Most people don't walk correctly with a straight spine and feet parallel to each other, and a few inches apart. Each step starts the cycle of lifting the foot a little way off the ground and placing the heel down first, then moving forward as the foot bends with the toes being last to leave the ground as the cycle begins again. It is all a gentle fluid rolling motion; with practice you can glide across the terrain, effortlessly, for mile after mile.

Short Circular walks
on the Grantham Canal

by Revd. John N. Merrill
THE JOHN MERRILL FOUNDATION

1

THE JOHN MERRILL FOUNDATION
32, Holmesdale, Waltham Cross,
Hertfordshire, England. EN8 8QY
Tel/Fax - 01992-762776
E-mail - john@johnmerrillwalkguides.co.uk
www. johnmerrillwalkguides.co.uk
www.thejohnmerrillministry.co.uk
www.londoninterfaithchurch.co.uk

A catalogue record for this book is available from the British Library.

Conceived, edited, typset and designed by *The John Merrill Foundation*
Printed and handmade by *John N. Merrill.*
Book layout and cover design by *John N. Merrill*

© Text and photographs - by Revd. John N. Merrill 2013
© Maps by Revd. John N. Merrill, HonMUniv, R.I.M.A. 2013
© Additional material - Revd. John N. Merrill, HonMUniv, 2013.

ISBN 978 - 1-903627-56-3
First Published - June 2004. Reprinted and revised - April 2013.
Special limited edition.

Typeset in Humanst521 - bold, italic, and plain 11pt, 14pt and 18pt
Main titles in 18pt .**Humanst521 Bd BT** by John Merrill in Adobe Pagemaker on a iMac.

Please note - *The maps in this guide are purely illustrative. You are encouraged to use the appropriate 1:25,000 O.S. Explorer map as detailed on each walk.*

John Merrill confirms he has walked all the routes in this book and detailed what he found. Meticulous research has been undertaken to ensure that this publication is highly accurate at the time of going to press. The publishers, however, cannot be held responsible for alterations, errors, omissions, or for changes in details given. They would welcome information to help keep the book up to date.

Cover design & photo's © The John Merrill Foundation 2013.
Photographs by Revd. John N. Merrill.

The John Merrill Foundation maintains the John Merrill Library and archives and administers the worldwide pubishing rights of John Merrill's works in all media formats.

Printed on paper from a 100% sustainable forest.
The John Merrill Foundation plants sufficient trees through the Woodland Trust to replenish the trees used in its publications.

John high up the mountain path, beside the Santa Barbara Chapel, overlooking Lake Garda, Italy.

A little about Revd. John N. Merrill

John is unique, possessing the skills of a marathon runner, mountain climber and athlete. Since his first 1,000 mile walk through the islands of the Inner and Outer Hebrides in 1970, he has since walked over 218,000 miles and worn out 132 paits of boots, 49 rucksacks and more than 1,600 pairs of socks. He has brought marathon walking to Olympic standard. In 1978 he became the first person to walk around the entire coastline of Britain - 7,000 miles. He has walked across Europe, the Alps and Pyrenees - 3,000 miles with 600,000 feet of ascent and descent. In America he has walked the 2,500 mile Appalachian Trail; the Pacific Crest Trail - 2,500 miles in record time; the Continental Divide Trail; became the first person to thru-hike the Buckeye Trail - 1,350 miles in Ohio and completed a unique 4,260 mile walk in 178 days coast to coast across America. He has climbed all the mountains in New Mexico and walked all the trails.

In Britain he has walked all the National Trails many times; linked all the National Parks and trails in a 2,060 mile walk; completed a 1,608 mile Land's End to John o' Groats walk and countless other unique walks. He has walked three times to Santiago de Compostella via different routes; to St. Olav's Shrine in Norway - 420 miles; walked to Assisi, St. Gilles du Gard, the Cathar Ways and to Mont St. Michel. He has walked every long distance path in France and Germany, and walked to every pilgrimage destination in England and France, and extensively walked in every country in Europe.

He has walked in Africa; all the trails in the Hong Kong Islands; and completed five trekking expeditions to the Himalyas and India. Not only is he the world's leading marathon walker he is Britain's most experienced walker. John is author of more than 440 walk guides which have sold more than 4 million copies with more than 1 million sold on the Peak District. He has created more than 80 challenge walks which have been used to raise, so far, more than a £1 million for different charities.

John has never broken a bone or been lost and never had any trouble anywhere. He still walks in the same body he was born with, has had no replacements and does not use poles. This he puts down to his deep spiritual nature and in 2010 he was ordained as a multi-faith Minister - a universal monk, "honouring and embracing all faiths and none". He conducts weddings and funerals services all over UK and abroad. He teaches Qigong and is a Reiki practioner.

CONTENTS

INTRODUCTION

Between the River Trent in Nottingham to Grantham runs the meandering thread of the Grantham Canal. I have walked it many times and even have a 25 mile challenge walk - The Belvoir Witches - that incorporates part of it. My wanderings have brought me to this peaceful canal and a whole host of fascinating and unspoilt villages that lie beside and close to it. I consider the canal to be one of the unforgotten walking areas of the East Midlands and rarely do I see another walker as I stride along. The scenery is most pleasant and gentle with the Vale of Belvoir, a stunning area.

These walks between 4 and 8 miles long interlock and completely explore the whole canal and surrounding villages. You can, if you wish, join two together making a pleasant day's walk or you could spend a weekend walking it end to end! Being canal walking there are no hills to climb and the miles simply flow by! As you walk the walks, you walk in parts of three counties Nottinghamshire, Leicestershire and finally Lincolnshire.

The beauty of these walks lies in the fascinating villages and the unspoilt countryside. Here time has stood still with quaint inns and historical churches. In spring the canal becomes alive as coots, moorhens, mallards, canada geese and mute swans prepare their nests. By late May the chicks are hatched and dutifully follow mother on the canal. There are still a few relics of the canal when it was in use. With bridges still showing the rope grooves from the horse rope, that pulled the narrow boat. Some locks have been restored while others lie derelict. And, unlike many canals you are never far from a mile post, stating how many miles you are from the Trent.

So, put your boots on and set off along the towpath and explore this tranquil heaven in beautiful countryside. You walk at the pace of the former narrow boats, that once brought coal and goods to Grantham and produce to Nottingham. It is a fascinating journey and world waiting to be visited.

Happy walking! John N. Merrill

ABOUT THE WALKS

Whilst every care is taken detailing and describing the walks ikn this book, it should be borne in mind that the countryside changes witgh the seasons and the work of man. I have described the walks to the best of my ability, detailing what I have found actually on the walk in the way of stiles, kissing gates and signs. You should always walk with the appropriate O.S. map as detailed for each walk; open on the walk area for constant reference, or downladed onto your mobile phone. Obviously with the passage of time stiles become broken or replaced by kissing gates; inns change their name or have close down. Signs have a habit of being broken or pushed over and often they are pointing in the wrong direction! All the routes follow public rights of way and only rarely will you find a tree blown down across the path or an electric fence, requiring a small detour. Some rights of way are rerouted such as around a farm but they are generally well signed.

All rights of way have colour coded arrows on marker posts, stiles, gates, path posts, trees and these help you showing the direction of travel.

YELLOW - Public footpath.
BLUE - Public bridleway.
RED - Byway open to all traffic (BOAT).
BLACK - Road used as a public path (RUPP).
WHITE - Concessionary and Permissive path.

The seasons bring occasional problems whilst out walking which should also be borne in mind. In the height of summer the paths become overgrown and you may have to fight your way through in a few places. In low lying areas the fields are full of crops. Usually a defined path leads through. In summer the ground is usually dry but in autumn and winter can be wet and slippery.

The mileage for each walk is based on several calculations -
1. My pedometer reading and steps taken - usually 2,000 to a mile.
2. The route on the map measured.
3. The time I took for the walk - the average person walks at 3mph - 2.5mph uphill.

Allow 20 mins for a mile; 10 mins for 1/2 mile and 5 mins for 1/4 mile.

"For every mile that you walk you extend your life by 21 mins."

8

Follow the Countryside Code.

* Be safe - plan ahead and follow any signs.

* Leave gates and property as you find them.

* Protect plants and animals, and take your litter home.

* Keep dogs under close control.

* Consider other people.

WALKING THE GRANTHAM CANAL

The canal is well marked and numbered. Unique among canals the Grantham Canal has mileposts every 1/4 mile from the River Trent. All the bridges are numbered from the River Trent and often have their names on. All locks are numbered from the Trent and many have their names on. At many road crossing are canal plaques showing where you are on the canal and mileage to the next place and to Nottingham and Grantham.

A canal milepost.

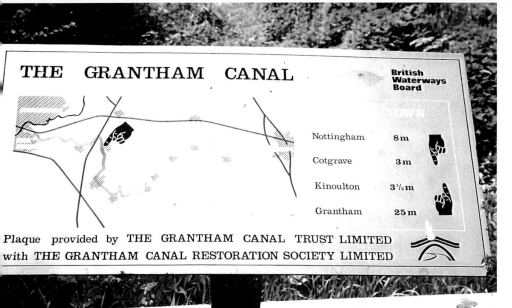

Roadside Canal plaque.

Bridge name and number.

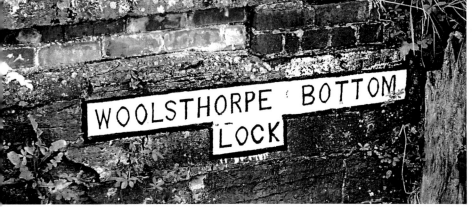

Lock name.

11

GRANTHAM CANAL
- Brief History Notes -

The main driving force for a canal was the cost of coal in Grantham. It was brought overland from the River Trent. A canal would bring in a much cheaper supply and enable the agricultural produce to be shipped out. At a single meeting £40,000 was raised for the canal construction.

William Jessop surveyed the line and two engineers saw to its construction. James Green was responsible for the section from the River Trent to the Leicestershire border, and William King from there to Grantham.

Authorised by Act of Parliament in 1793.

Built at a cost £118,500 and after four years was opened in 1797. The canal rose 139 ft. 9 inches to Grantham via eighteen locks. There were 67 swing bridges and nine small aqueducts.

The canal ran from the River Trent, Nottingham, opposite the lock entrance of the Nottingham Canal, and ran for 33 miles, through Nottinghamshire, Leicestershire and Lincolnshire to Earle's Field Lane, Grantham.

In 1936 the canal was abandoned by Act of Parliament.

Between Lock 12 near Muston Bridge No. 59 and Lock 11 in Nottinghamshire, the pound is 20 miles long; one of the longest on any canal.

The canal transported agricultural goods and brought back coal, roof slates, lime and fertiliser. There was a Coal Wharf behind the Peacock inn in Redmile. In the early 1900's the publican was described as being, "A farmer, victualler and coal dealer." In 1841 the canal toll receipts reached there highest point of £13,079. With the opening of the Nottingham - Grantham Railway in 1850, the canal transport was dramatically reduced. The dividend on shares which had often been £10 now fell to £2. By 1861 the canal was owned by the Railway Company. Boats with coal from the Erewash area came down the Erewash Canal or Nottingham Canal and reached Grantham five days later. After 1880 the canal ran at a loss and by 1929 was closed to traffic. In 1905 the total tonnage carried on the canal was 18,802 tons and by 1924 this had fallen to 1,583 tons. Today there only a few swing bridges left, and most of the hump backed bridges have been removed, leaving only handful of the original bridges in place.

The first lock and start of the Grantham Canal by the River Trent. Behind can be seen part of the Nottingham Forest Football Ground stand.

THE RIVER TENT AND START OF THE GRANTHAM CANAL - 8 MILES

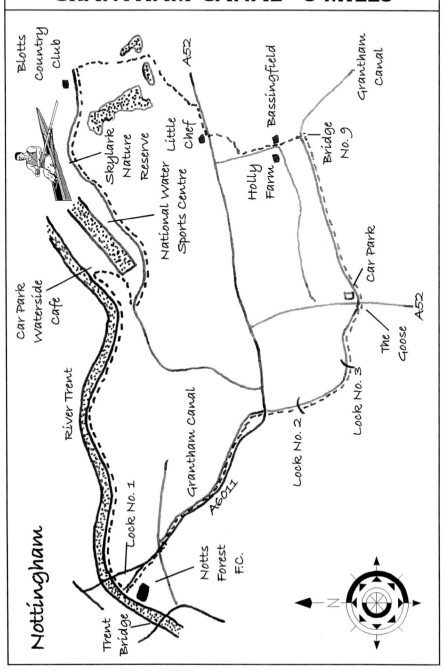

Blotts Country Club

Skylark Nature Reserve

A52

Little Chef

Bassingfield

Grantham Canal

Bridge No. 9

Holly Farm

National Water Sports Centre

Car Park

Car Park

Waterside Cafe

The Goose

A52

River Trent

Grantham Canal

Lock No. 2

Lock No. 3

Lock No. 1

A6011

Notts Forest F.C.

Nottingham

Trent Bridge

N

THE RIVER TRENT AND START OF THE GRANTHAM CANAL
- 8 MILES
- allow 3 hours or more.

Basic Route - Tollerton Road Car park - Grantham Canal - Bridge No. 9 - Bassingfield - A52 & Little Chef - Holme Pierrepont - Adbolton Lane - Trent Valley Way - National Water Sports Centre - Car park - River Trent - Lock 1 Grantham Canal - Grantham Canal - Tollerton Road Car park.

Map - O.S. 1:25,000 Explorer Series No. 260 - Nottingham & Vale of Belvoir - West Sheet.

Car Park and start - Tollerton Road, off the A52, by Bridge No. 7. Grid Ref. 608368. Alternative start and car park at the National Water Sports Centre - Grid Ref. 609389.

Inns - The Goose by A52.

Teas - Little Chef by A52. BP Garage shop. Waterside cafe, National Water sports Centre, public car park.

ABOUT THE WALK - Starting from Tollerton Road you follow the canal eastwards for a mile before heading northwards to Holme Pierrepont and the River Trent. Heading westwards now, you walk beside the river for two miles to the Nottingham Forest Football ground and the first lock and start of the Grantham Canal. You now follow the canal for nearly three miles past houses back into quiet countryside. Much of the canal is still visible and water filled, and you pass two abandoned locks. On the walk you explore two modes of water transport, the navigable River Trent and Grantham Canal.

WALKING INSTRUCTIONS - From the car park beside Tollerton Road, turn right to the canal and towpath on its righthand side. Follow the canal eastwards for more than a mile past bridge No. 8 and onto bridge No. 9. Here leave the canal and turn left along a track to the houses of Bassingfield and lane. Gaining the lane with Holly Farm opposite, keep straight ahead past it on Bassingfield Lane for 1/4 mile to a footpath sign on your right. Turn right and keep the hedge on your left to a stile on your left. Cross the corner of the next field to a stile and bear left to the A52 opposite the Little Chef and BP petrol station. Take care crossing the main road and turn right and in 250 yards left at a footpath sign and stile. First walk along a concrete path and in 100 yards, as path arrowed turn right and walk around the edge of the field into woodland and a track. The track becomes fenced and follow it and in 1/4 mile left between lakes and on to the road at Holme Pierrepont. The path turns left and parallels the road before crossing a wooden footbridge to gain the road opposite Blotts Country Club entrance. Please note this path line from the A52 to here is further east than shown on the O.S. map, having been diverted through the sand and gravel pits.

Turn left along the road - Adbolton Lane - now following the Trent Valley Way. Pass the Skylark Nature Reserve on your right and more than 1 mile later, where the road turns left, turn right on the Water Sports road, with a cricket ground on your left, to the car park and Waterside Cafe beside the River Trent; a Trent Valley Way sign is at the start of the road, pointing in the direction you have come from. Walk along the lefthand side of the car park to another large Trent Valley Way sign, and turn left now walking along the banks of the River Trent. Pass the 1 3/4 mile marker, then the Nottingham Sailing Club House on your left. Continue by the river for the next 1 1/2 miles passing the 2 km and 1 Km markers. Opposite the latter on the other side of the river can be seen the former British Waterways Warehouses and boat docks. Continue and pass under the A6011 road and just after reach the first lock and start of the Grantham Canal.

Turn left to walk along the towpath with the canal on your left to the A6011 road. Follow it to Lady Bay Bridge (no bridge) and road junction.

16

Aptly on your right is the Grantham Hotel. Keep straight ahead along the A6011 road and in 100 yards on your left rejoin the canal towpath. In nearly 1/2 mile cross Rutland Road and keep ahead along the A6011 road a short distance before turning left to regain the canal. The road soon turns away from the canal and you pass under Gamston Bridge - No. 4. Continue beside the canal and pass Lock No. 2, then Bridge No. 5 and onto Lock No. 3 and Bridge No. 6. The canal now swings left then right to a road and the A52 ahead, with The Goose Inn on the right. Cross to the A52 road; opposite can be seen the handrail and steps to continue on the canal towpath. To get there it is best to turn left beside the road to the junction of the Tollerton Road, on the right. Cross with care and turn right along the other side to the steps down to rejoin the canal. Follow it to Tollerton Road and car park on your left.

National Water Sports Centre.

The Navigable River Trent.

The Grantham Canal beside the A6011.

Lock No. 2

Lock No. 3

COTGRAVE AND THE GRANTHAM CANAL - 5 MILES

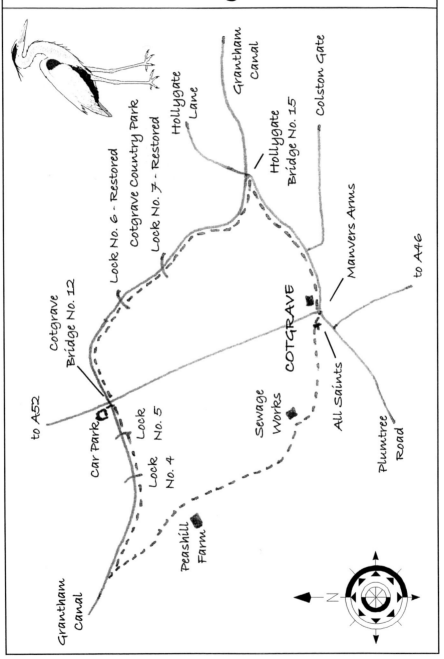

COTGRAVE AND THE GRANTHAM CANAL
- 5 MILES
- allow 2 or more hours.

Basic Route - Cotgrave Bridge Car Park - Grantham Canal - Hollygate Bridge No. 15 - Cotgrave - All Saints Church - Sewage Works - Peashill Farm - Grantham Canal - Locks 4 and 5 - Cotgrave Bridge car park.

O.S. MAP

Map - O.S. 1:25,000 Explorer Series No. 260 - Nottingham & Vale of Belvoir - East Sheet.

VISITOR PARKING

Car park and start - Cotgrave Bridge No. 12, beside the A52 - Cotgrave road. Grid Ref. 638367.

Inns - Manvers Arms, Cotgrave.

ABOUT THE WALK - A delightful walk along a restored section of the canal, past Locks No. 6 and 7 restored in May 2,000. The surrounding area is now Cotgrave Country Park, formerly part of Cotgrave Colliery - 1964 - 1993. Leaving the canal you follow the road into Cotgrave and its church dedicated to All Saints. A path from here leads over the fields past Peashill Farm back to the canal. Here by way of contrast you pass two locks - Nos. 4 and 5 - which await restoration, before regaining the car park. There is a short one mile circular bicentenary walk - 1793-1993 - that you can follow both sides of the canal between the car park and Lock No. 4. On the canal swans, coots and moorhens nest and in the fields the song of the skylark can be head. Grey Herons stand motionlessly beside the canal waiting for a fish. You will no doubt see light aircraft taking off and landing at Nottingham Airport. The airport was officially opened by the Lord Mayor of Nottingham in 1929; the year the canal closed.

WALKING INSTRUCTIONS - Cross the road from the car park and gain the canal towpath with the canal on your left; behind you is your return path. Follow the restored canal for little over 1/2 mile to Lock No. 6, the first restored lock. 1/4 mile later reach restored Lock No. 7. Not long after pass the canal milepost - 5 miles to the Trent. These canal mileposts are a feature of this canal and are often every 1/4 mile. Continue another 1/2 mile to Hollygate Bridge No. 15, with milepost 5 1/2 miles just beyond. Here gain Hollygate Lane and turn right and follow the road for 1/2 mile into central Cotgrave.

At the main road junction with the Manvers Arms on the left and All Saints church and cross shaft opposite, walk along Church Lane on the immediate right of the church. At The Limes, turn right as path signed - Tollerton 2 miles - and follow the walled path to a field. Turn left and follow the path to the top left side and a metal gate. Keep straight ahead on a former lane to a stile and continue with the hedge on your right to a track and sewage works on the right. Turn right and follow the track as it swings left to a solitary factory. Before it keep right to a gate and continue on the path by a hedge on the left. Reach another gate and soon afterwards cross the farm track to Peashill Farm on the left. Keep ahead now on a track which in 1/2 mile brings you back to the Grantham Canal. Turn right and follow the canal for a mile past the abandoned locks No. 4 - Skinner's Lock - and No. 5 back to Cotgrave Bridge No. 12 and car park on the left. You can from Lock 4 walk on the otherside of the canal back to the car park.

5 miles from Trent, canal milepost.

Lock No. 7 - restored May 2000.

Lock No. 5.

COTGRAVE AND CROPWELL BISHOP
- 8 MILES

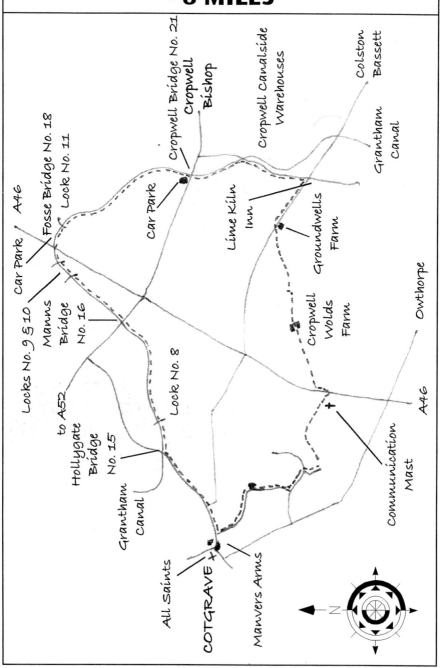

Cropwell Bridge No. 21

Cropwell Bishop

Cropwell Canalside Warehouses

Colston Bassett

Grantham Canal

Fosse Bridge No. 18

Lock No. 11

Car Park

Lime Kiln Inn

Groundwells Farm

A46

Car Park

Locks No. 9 & 10

Car Park

Manns Bridge No. 16

Cropwell Wolds Farm

Owthorpe

Lock No. 8

A46

to A52

Communication Mast

Hollygate Bridge No. 15

Grantham Canal

All Saints

COTGRAVE

Manvers Arms

N

CROPWELL BISHOP
AND COTGRAVE
- 8 MILES
- allow 3 or more hours.

Basic Route - Fosse Bridge (No. 18) Car Park - Grantham Canal - Cropwell Bridge - Lime Kiln Inn - Groundwells Farm - Cropwell Wolds Farm - A46 (Fosse Way) - Cotgrave Gorse - Cotgrave - Hollygate Bridge No. 15 - Grantham Canal - Fosse Bridge.

Map - O.S. 1:25,000 Explorer Series No. 260 - Nottingham & the Vale of Belvoir.

Car park and start - Fosse Bridge (No. 18) beside the A46 at Grid Ref. 674368. Picnic table here. Alternative car park at Cropwell Bridge No. 21; Grid Ref. 678355.

Inns - Lime Kiln Inn, south of Cropwell Bishop and on the route. Manvers Arms just off the route in Cotgrave. One in Cropwell Bishop village, 1/2 mile from route.

ABOUT THE WALK - You follow a large loop of the canal with the Fosse Bridge at the top. Beyond Cropwell Bishop you pass near former canalside industrial buildings - Cropwell Wharf, before crossing the Cropwell Wolds with extensive views, before descending to Cotgrave. A walk through the town takes you past the monument of Cotgrave Colliery - 1964 - 1993. A short road walk returns you back to the canal at Hollygate Bridge No. 15, leaving two miles of canal walking, passed ruined locks and dry canal back to Fosse Bridge.

WALKING INSTRUCTIONS - From the end of the car park at Fosse Bridge, cross a footbridge over Lock No. 11 and gain the towpath. Turn left and walk beside the canal on your left. Keep beside the canal for more than a mile passing bridges No. 19 and 20. Much of the canal here is dry as you pass mileposts - 7 1/4 and 7 1/2 miles from the Trent. Gain Cropwell Bridge No. 21 and road to Cropwell Bishop. There is a car park on the left and 1/2 mile in the village is an inn. Cross the road and continue beside the dry canal to the next road 1/2 mile away. Here leave the canal and turn right onto a path close to the road. In a short distance to your left can be seen some excellent canalside industrial buildings - the former Cropwell Wharf. Continue on the path near a crossroads with the Lime Kiln Inn ahead. Follow the path right for more than 1/4 mile paralleling the Colston Road, to gain the road opposite Groundwells Farm. Cross to your right to a gate and path sign. Keep to the righthand edge of the field as you ascend to a field gap and onto a stile. You are now on the top of the Cropwell Wolds with 360° views.

Continue ahead to a farm track and turn left then right along it to Cropwell Wolds Farm. Walk past the buildings and house, turning left then right to continue on a track that leads straight to the A46 and steps down to it. Turn left and in a few yards right onto a track to a gate. Pass through and aim towards the prominent communications mast to your left and gain a track/path along the lefthand side of a wood. Follow the path down Cotgrave Gorse bearing left to the houses of Cotgrave. Keep left past the houses to Hickling Way and turn right along it to Furlong Way. Turn left and at a red P.O. pillar box, turn right along Woodview. Follow this past Cotgrave Welfare on the left and Cotgrave Leisure Centre on the right. Follow the road round to your left passing the winding wheel and three tubs from Cotgrave Colliery on the right. Continue on the road, now Candelby Lane to the main road in Cotgrave. To your left is the Manvers Arms and All Saints church.

Turn right along the road - Hollygate Lane - for more than 1/2 mile to Hollygate Bridge No. 15 and canal. Turn right and follow the canal towpath with the canal on your left, with water and reeds. Pass the ruined Lock No. 8 and milepost - 5 3/4 miles. After a mile from the road reach Mann's Bridge No. 16 and Nottingham Road, from Cropwell Bishop. Continue beside the canal for 3/4 mile, at first reed filled then dry, passing the ruined Locks No. 9 and 10 before passing under Fosse Bridge, No. 18. Continue to Lock No. 11 and cross the footbridge back to the car park.

CROPWELL BISHOP - St. Giles church dates from the 13th (1215) and 14th. century with the tower being built in the 15th. century.

COTGRAVE - All Saints church has traces of Norman times; with the tower and spire are 14th. century.

The Cotgrave and Cropwell Bishop walk can be joined together as one long walk of approximately 12 miles.

Cotgrave Colliery - 1964 - 1993.

Fosse Bridge, car park and Lock No. 11.

Former Cropwell Wharf.

The dry canal and dandelion lined towpath.

Ruined lock.

MACKLEY'S BRIDGE AND OWTHORPE - 6 MILES

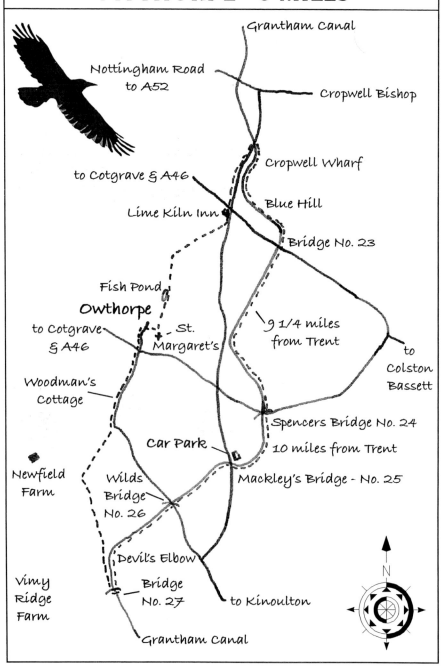

Grantham Canal

Nottingham Road
to A52

Cropwell Bishop

Cropwell Wharf

to Cotgrave & A46

Blue Hill

Lime Kiln Inn

Bridge No. 23

Fish Pond

Owthorpe

to Cotgrave
& A46

St.
Margaret's

9 1/4 miles
from Trent

to
Colston
Bassett

Woodman's
Cottage

Spencers Bridge No. 24

Car Park

10 miles from Trent

Newfield
Farm

Wilds
Bridge
No. 26

Mackley's Bridge - No. 25

Devil's Elbow

Vimy
Ridge
Farm

Bridge
No. 27

to Kinoulton

N

Grantham Canal

MACKLEY'S BRIDGE AND OWTHORPE
- 6 MILES
- allow 2 1/2 hours.

Basic Route - Mackley's Bridge Car Park - Grantham Canal - Devil's Elbow - Bridge No. 27 (Poplar Avenue) - Owthorpe - Fish Ponds - Lime Kiln Inn - Cropwell Wharf - Grantham Canal - Mackley's Bridge.

Map - O.S. 1:25,000 Explorer Series No. 260 - Nottingham & Vale of Belvoir.

Car Park and start - beside Mackley's Bridge No. 25 on the Grantham Canal. Grid Ref. 679325. Picnic tables.

Inn - Lime Kiln Inn on the Colston Road.

ABOUT THE WALK - Impressive canal walking brings you past the sharp canal bend known as the Devil's Elbow. Soon after you leave the canal at Bridge No. 27, opposite Vimy Ridge Farm and 184 Poplar trees. You walk along the otherside of the canal before crossing the fields to the Owthorpe Road. Owthorpe is a fascinating hamlet with an unusual church, just off the route. You continue northwards past fish ponds, to rejoin the canal beyond the Lime Kiln Inn, at Cropwell Wharf. Here you follow the canal southwards for 1 1/2 miles back to the car park.

WALKING INSTRUCTIONS - At Mackley's Bridge car park cross the road to the canal on the right, and begin following the towpath with the water filled canal on your right. The canal to your left, from the "bridge

31

(No. 25)", is your return path. Pass canal milepost, "10 1/4 mile from the Trent". In little over 1/4 mile cross the road at Wild's Bridge No. 26, and continue beside the canal on your right. Soon the canal turns sharp left at the Devil's Elbow; opposite you will soon be walking along a path there. Follow the canal to the next bridge, No. 27., and turning circle on the right. On your left is the row of 184 Poplar trees and to your right is Vimy Ridge Farm; see history notes below. Turn right across the canal bridge and immediately turn right down steps to walk along the other side of the canal on a small path. At the Devil's Elbow follow the path through a cluster of trees and the otherside is a stile on your left. Follow the path with a hedge on your left to a wooden footbridge. Keep ahead with a ditch on your left to the farm track to Newfield Farm and path and bridleway sign. Turn right along the track to the Owthorpe road. Keep straight ahead along the road passing Woodman's Cottage on your left and onto the crossroads before Owthorpe village.

Go straight across and walk into the hamlet of Owthorpe and in a short distance right along the grass track to Owthorpe church, dedicated to St. Margaret. In a few yards on your left is a stile and your next path; but before taking it it is worth visiting the church. At the stile cross the field to far lefthand corner to a stile. Turn left to another stile and continue heading northwards as you gently descend the field to the immediate right of Fish Ponds. Reach a stile and continue past the pond on your left to another stile. Continue with the hedge on your left to a footbridge. Bear half right across the next field to a stile and onto another, with a farm to your right. Cross leftwards the farmyard to a stile and road. Turn left to the crossroads and the Lime Kiln Inn on your left. At the crossroads, cross the lefthand side of the grass to a gap on the hedge and gain a path gate and path. Turn right and follow the path which parallels the road, for 1/4 mile, to regain the Cropwell Bishop road, with the Grantham Canal and Cropwell Wharf on the right. Turn left and in a few yards right, at Roving Bridge No. 22, to regain the canal. Pass the canalside, Cropwell Wharf on the left, walking beside a mostly dry canal bed on your right. The canal soon swings left and later right to the Colston road at Bridge No. 23. Continue beside the reed and water filled canal, passing canal milepost - 9 1/4 miles to Trent. The canal becomes a dry bed again and in 1/2 mile reach Spencer's Bridge No. 24. Cross over and continue beside the now water filled canal for more than 1/4 mile to Mackley's Bridge No. 25. At the road turn right back to the car park.

184 POPLAR TREES - The avenue of trees was originally planted by Sir William Hind, in memory of his son, Francis Montagu Hind, who was killed during the Battle of the Somme on the 27th. September 1916. The other 183 trees are in memory of the other 183 officers from the Sherwood Forester Regiment who also died during the battle between 7th. July and 30th. November 1916, the end of the battle. The British only advanced eight miles during the battle and suffered some 600,000 casualties; one of the bloodiest battles of World War One. Vimy Ridge Farm is named after a ridge in the battleground, where Francis Montagu Hind was killed.

OWTHORPE - The church, dedicated to St. Margaret, was restored in 1705; the tower clock dates from the 18th century.

In the 17th. century there once stood a large hall built by the Hutchinson family. At the time of Civil War, Colonel John Hutchinson was the Puritan Governor of Nottingham. Owthorpe Hall was destroyed by the Cavaliers and Colonel Hutchinson was imprisoned. He died in prison in 1664 and lies buried in the church. The hall was rebuilt and later sold in 1773 before becoming ruinous once more.

Canal, swans nest and turning circle at Bridge No. 27, at the Poplar Avenue.

Martins Arms, Colston Bassett.

MACKLEY'S BRIDGE, KINOULTON AND COLSTON BASSETT - 6 MILES

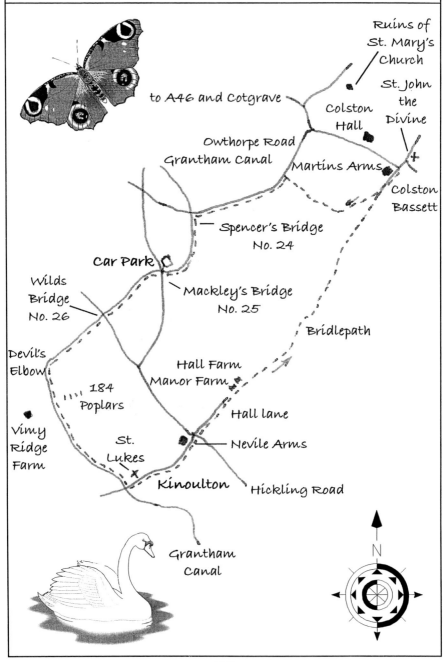

Ruins of
St. Mary's
Church

St. John
the
Divine

to A46 and Cotgrave

Colston
Hall

Owthorpe Road
Grantham Canal

Martins Arms

Colston
Bassett

Spencer's Bridge
No. 24

Car Park

Wilds
Bridge
No. 26

Mackley's Bridge
No. 25

Bridlepath

Devil's
Elbow

Hall Farm
Manor Farm

184
Poplars

Vimy
Ridge
Farm

Hall Lane

St.
Lukes

Nevile Arms

Kinoulton

Hickling Road

Grantham
Canal

N

MACKLEY'S BRIDGE, KINOULTON AND COLSTON BASSETT
- 6 MILES
- allow 2 1/2 hours.

Basic route - Mackley's Bridge Car Park - Grantham Canal - Devil's Elbow - Kinoulton - Hall Farm - River Smite - Colston Bassett - Owthorpe Road - Spencer's Bridge - Grantham Canal - Mackley's Bridge Car Park.

O.S. MAP

Map - O.S. 1:25,000 Explorer Series No. 260 - Nottingham & Vale of Belvoir.

VISITOR PARKING

Car park and start - beside Mackley's Bridge No. 25, on the Grantham Canal. Grid Ref. 679325. Picnic tables.

Inns - Nevile Arms, Kinoulton. Martins Arms, Colston Bassett.

ABOUT THE WALK - First you walk a couple of miles along the Grantham Canal to Kinoulton - Bridge No. 26. Leaving the canal you walk through Kinoulton village and onto the bridlepath to Colston Bassett. The route does not take you all the way into the village, but it is well worth a visit to see the cross and church and an inn! You cross the field to Owthorpe Road and soon regain the canal for the final 1/2 mile back to the car park.

WALKING INSTRUCTIONS - Cross the road to the right to gain the canal. The first part is delightful water filled section, with swans gliding by. Pass canal mileposts 10 1/4 and 10 1/2 miles from the Trent. Cross the

37

Owthorpe lane at Wild's Bridge No. 26, and continue beside the canal on your right and soon left around d the Devil's Elbow. Soon afterwards cross the track at Bridge No. 27, to Vimy Ridge Farm and the Poplar Avenue on the left. Continue beside the canal and in more than 1/2 mile reach Bridge No. 28 and the road at Kinoulton. Leave the canal here and turn left to walk through the village passing St. Luke's church on your left. In 1/2 mile reach the Hickling Road, with Nevile Arms on the left.

Go straight across into Hall Lane and follow it past the Post Office. Continue on the lane - a no through road - passing Manor Farm on your left and later Hall Farm; here the lane ends. Keep straight ahead through a gate and now on a bridlepath. Keep the fence on your left. Pass under electricity cables before bearing slightly left to reach a gate and footbridge. Keep to the righthand side of the field by a hedge and River Smite. Follow around the field edge, eventually turning left to a gate beside a wood. Continue with the hedge and fence on your right eventually reaching a gate with Colston Bassett village ahead. Continue to the village lane and on your left, opposite Angel Cottage is the stile and path sign, for Owthorpe Road. Before taking it keep ahead to visit the village.

At the stile bear slightly right and cross the middle of the field to two gates and bridge. To your right can be seen the white painted Colston Hall. Bear right across the lefthand side of the field to a gate and track. Follow the track to the Owthorpe Road. Turn left and follow the road for more than 1/2 mile to the canal at Spencer's Bridge No. 24. Turn left and follow the canal passing milepost - 10 miles from Trent - and onto Mackley's Bridge. Turn right back to the car park.

COLSTON HALL - the white painted hall was built in 1704 in classical Italianate style. An orangery and further alterations took place in the 1860's.

KINOULTON - The red bricked classical style church. dedicated to St. Luke, was built by Henry, Earl of Gainsborough in 1795.

Market Cross, Colston Bassett.

St. John the Divine.

COLSTON BASSETT - The Market Cross is National Trust property. Opposite on the garden wall of the Martins Arms can be seen a plaque to a tree in the grounds. Planted to commemorate the 100th. birthday of Mrs. Emily Bint - 20th. January 1988.

To the north of the village is the ruins of St. Mary's church. This decayed and was later made roofless. A new church dedicated to St. John the Divine, was dedicated on the 2nd. August 1892. The church is built in early perpendicular style and designed by Arthur Brewill of Nottingham. For such a small village it is a splendid building with the tower forming part of the chancel. Inside are many carved roof angels, and the Knowles Chapel. Some bells and monuments are from St. Mary's church. The spire rises to 150 feet and is a useful landmark in the area.

Hickling Canal Basin and Plough Inn.

HICKLING, KINOULTON & COLSTON BASSETT - 7 MILES

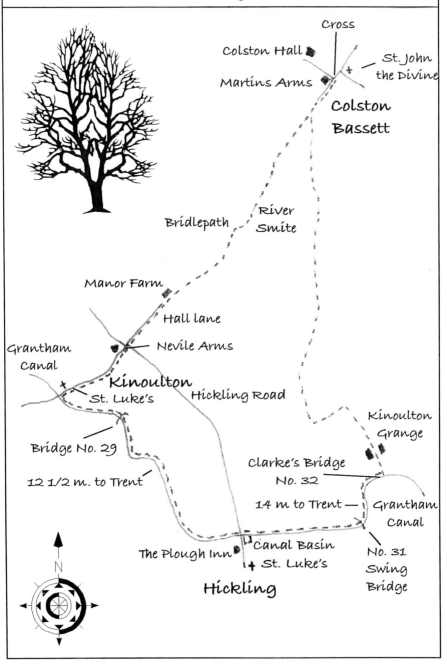

Cross

Colston Hall

St. John
the Divine

Martins Arms

Colston
Bassett

River
Smite

Bridlepath

Manor Farm

Hall lane

Grantham
Canal

Nevile Arms

Kinoulton

St. Luke's

Hickling Road

Kinoulton
Grange

Bridge No. 29

12 1/2 m. to Trent

Clarke's Bridge
No. 32

14 m to Trent

Grantham
Canal

The Plough Inn

Canal Basin

St. Luke's

Hickling

No. 31
Swing
Bridge

N

HICKLING, KINOULTON &
COLSTON BASSETT
- 7 MILES
- allow 3 hours.

Basic route - Hickling - Grantham Canal - Kinoulton - Hall Farm - River Smite - Colston Bassett - Kinoulton Grange - Clarke's Bridge No. 32 - Grantham Canal - Hickling.

Map - O.S. 1:25,000 Explorer Series No. 260 - Nottingham & Vale of Belvoir.

Car park and start - Roadside parking at Hickling. Grid Ref. 692294.

Inns - The Plough Inn, Hickling. Nevile Arms, Kinoulton. Martins Arms, Colston Bassett.

ABOUT THE WALK - Starting from the stunning canalside location at Hickling in Leicestershire, with its canal basin, you follow the canal north-westerly to Kinoulton. Walking through the village you pass the church and inn before following a bridlepath to the small but historically interesting Colston Bassett, Nottinghamshire, which just off the route but well worth a visit. Turning southwards you follow a path to Kinoulton Grange and regain the canal at Clarke's Bridge - No. 32 - the first original canal bridge from the River Trent. All except for the Fosse Bridge on the A46 have been levelled. A mile of water filled canal walking takes you past the first Swing Bridge No. 31 on the canal, before regaining Hickling and its canal basin.

43

WALKING INSTRUCTIONS - From the canal at Hickling, at Bridge No. 30, turn left onto the towpath and walk beside canal on your left. Follow the canal for more than a mile, passing Canal Milepost - 13 and 12 miles from Trent. At bridge No. 28, turn right into Kinoulton. Pass St. Luke's church on your left and 1/2 mile later the Nevile Arms on your left at the Hickling Road crossroads. Go straight across into Hall Lane and pass the Post Office on your right. Continue on the No Through Road, past Manor Farm and onto Hall Farm at the end of the lane. Keep straight ahead through a gate by a bridlepath sign. Keep a fence on your left, then pass under electric cables and follow the path slightly left to reach a gate and footbridge. Continue with a hedge on your right and the River Smite. Keep to the righthand side of the field for 1/2 mile before following it left to a gate and small wood on the left. Continue ahead on the righthand side of the field by the fence and hedge to a gate well before the houses of Colston Bassett. Here on the right is a stile and path sign, your next path to the canal more than two miles away. But first it is worth continuing into Colston Bassett village to see the church, market cross, and Martins Arms.

Retrace your steps back to the gate, stile and path sign. The path goes diagonally across the middle of the field to a stile and footbridge. Cross and bear left along the field edge beside the hedge to another footbridge on your left. Cross and keep to the righthand side of the field with a stream on your right and in 1/4 mile gain a stile and electric cables above. Walk around the righthand corner of the field to a footbridge and continue with field hedge on your right to another footbridge more than 1/4 mile away. You can see Kinoulton Grange ahead but your route is not direct as it bear right and left. Keep the hedge on your right and soon pass under the electric pylon cables. Follow the field edge round to your left to reach a farm track. Turn right and follow the concrete drive to Kinoulton Grange. Walk straight through between the buildings and keep ahead on a track which brings you to Clarke's Bridge - No. 32 - and the Grantham Canal. Admire the view before descending steps on the right of the bridge down to the canal. Turn right and follow the canal for a mile back to Hickling and its canal basin. Pass the 14 miles from Trent milepost and the Swing Bridge No. 31. More than 1/2 mile later regain Hickling.

KINOULTON - Formerly part of the Gainsborough estate. The Nevile Arms on the inn show the Nevile and Noel arms, who were once the Earls of Gainsborough.

COLSTON BASSETT MARKET CROSS - 15th century sandstone base with a limestone shaft erected to commemorate the coronation of William IV in 1831.

MARTINS ARMS, COLSTON BASSETT - Early 18th century building and named after Henry Martin who was the owner of the Manor in the 19th century.

Clarke's Bridge No. 32.

Swing Bridge No. 31.

The canal at Hickling.

St. Luke's church, Hickling.

HICKLING - On the southern side of the Canal Basin is a canal warehouse built in the late 18th. century. Goods were unloaded and loaded here. St. Luke's church tower has 14th. century material in it. A former Rector was Ralph Babington, who died in 1521, was an ancestor of the Babington family who were involved in the infamous plot to rescue Mary Queen of Scots. His father is buried in Ashover church in Derbyshire. They once owned halls in Ashover and nearby Dethick. The graveyard contains many fine 18th century slate gravestones with delicate lettering and are worth reading.

COLSTON BASSETT AND LONG CLAWSON BRIDGE - 8 MILES

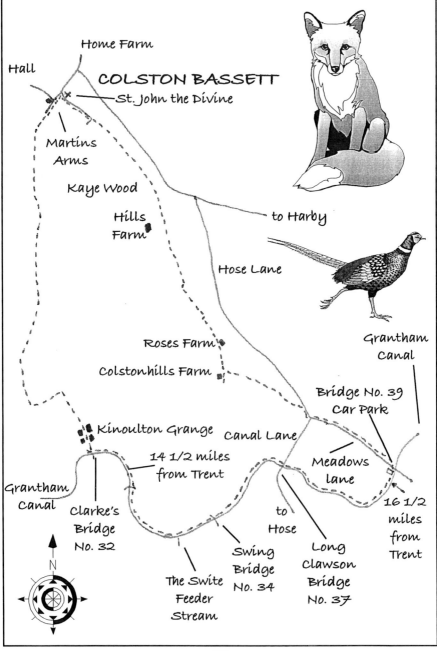

Home Farm

Hall

COLSTON BASSETT

St. John the Divine

Martins Arms

Kaye Wood

Hills Farm

to Harby

Hose Lane

Roses Farm

Colstonhills Farm

Grantham Canal

Bridge No. 39 Car Park

Kinoulton Grange

Canal Lane

14 1/2 miles from Trent

Meadows Lane

Grantham Canal

Clarke's Bridge No. 32

The Swite Feeder Stream

Swing Bridge No. 34

to Hose

Long Clawson Bridge No. 37

16 1/2 miles from Trent

N

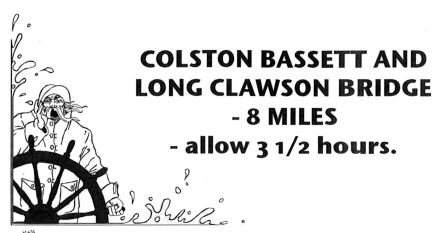

COLSTON BASSETT AND LONG CLAWSON BRIDGE
- 8 MILES
- allow 3 1/2 hours.

Basic Route - Bridge No. 39 (Meadows Lane) - Colstonhills Farm - Roses Farm - Hills Farm - Kaye Wood - Colston Bassett - Kinoulton Grange - Clarke's Bridge No. 32 - Grantham Canal - Bridge No. 39.

Map - O.S. 1:25,000 Explorer Series No. 260 - Nottingham & the Vale of Belvoir.

Car Park and start - Bridge No. 39 on Meadows Lane near Hose. Grid Ref. 732298. Alternative - limited roadside in Colston Bassett village.

Inn - Martins Arms, Colston Bassett; approximately halfway.

ABOUT THE WALK - Three walks radiate out from Colston Bassett with this one being the eastern one. Much of the walk is in Nottinghamshire with the start and end in Leicestershire. The route follows 2 1/2 miles of canal with footpath walking to and from Colston Bassett on well stiled paths, which are little used. Whilst I saw a lot of wildlife on the canal, I saw more on these quiet paths. Near Kaye Wood I surprised a fox, who after a few yards stopped and looked at me! Moments later I flushed a pheasant. I saw many hares and in one field I found a black sheep trapped in the mesh fence by its horns. He remained quite still while I twisted his head to unhook him from the wire. Free, he backed away before baa-ing loudly! Later I saw a swan on its nest get up and push her head down into the warm reeds to lift her three eggs individually, before settling down again in incubate her cygnets. These are some of joys of walking in the countryside and around each corner you have no idea what lies ahead. Clarke's Bridge no. 32 is a fine brick canal bridge. Later you pass two large canal swing bridges, used by farmers. The small village of Colston Bassett has an interesting cross and church, whose spire is a useful landmark for part of the route.

WALKING INSTRUCTIONS - From the car park beside Bridge No. 39, head north-westerly along Meadows Lane, away from the canal, passing Bridge House on your right. 1/2 mile later reach the junction with Canal Lane on your left and Hose Lane to Colston Bassett on the right. Turn right and in a few yards step into Nottinghamshire. A few yards later on your left is a gate, stile and footpath sign. Cross the middle of the field to a yellow topped post and on across the next field to a stile. Cross the next large field in the middle aiming for the righthand side of Colstonhills Farm. At the field hedge below the farm, well to your right is a brick pill box. Keep ahead with the hedge on your left and pass a pond before gaining the farm track. Cross to a footpath sign and stile. Cross the righthand side of the field to Roses Farm, turning left along the field edge to two gates. Continue with woodland on your left to a gate and on with a hedge on your left. Go through the gate on your right and continue with the hedge still on your left, to a footbridge.

Keep straight ahead along the field edge following right for a few yards at the end to reach the next stile. Continue with the hedge on your left to a stile and wooded strip on your left. Cross the middle of the next field to a stile and onto another with Hills Farm to your left. Continue with a hedge to your right to the farm track. Go straight across to a footbridge and continue across the middle of the field, paralleling Kaye Wood on your left. Reach another footbridge and ascend gently through the middle of the field to a gate gap. Continue straight ahead in the middle of the field, aiming towards the spire of Colston Bassett church, which has been a good landmark for this section of the route. Descend gently to a stile and path sign and lane, Bunnison Lane. Follow the lane into Colston Bassett and main road with the church, dedicated to St. John the Divine, on your right. Turn left to the market cross and left again to pass the Martins Arms on your right.

Follow the lane past Angel Cottage on your left. Keep ahead along the track to a gate. Just before it turn left over a stile. Go diagonally across the field to a stile and footbridge. Turn left and keep the hedge on your left to the next footbridge. Cross and turn right and keep a stream on your right for more than 1/4 mile to a stile, passing under electric cables. Cross the corner of the field to another footbridge and keep the hedge on your right. Basically for the next mile keep to the righthand side of the fields. In more than 1/4 mile cross a track to a footbridge and keep to the righthand side of the field by the hedge. Ignore two paths to your right as you pass under the electric cables again and follow the field edge round to your left. Reach the farm concrete drive and turn right to Kinoulton Grange. Keep straight ahead between the buildings and continue on a track to Clarke's Bridge, No. 32, and the canal. Before the bridge bear right and descend steps to the towpath. Turn left to walk under bridge.

Keep the canal on your right for the next 2 1/2 miles back to the car park at Bridge No. 39. Pass milepost - 14 1/4 miles from Trent - then Swing Bridge No. 33. Next the Smite Feeder No. 5, then Swing Bridge No. 34 and back into Leicestershire. 1/2 mile later cross the road at Bridge No 37 - Long Clawson Bridge. Continue by the canal passing bridge No. 38 and canal milepost - 16 1/2 miles from the Trent - the halfway point of the canal and just after regain Bridge No. 39, where you began.

The halfway point of the canal.

HARBY - 7 MILES

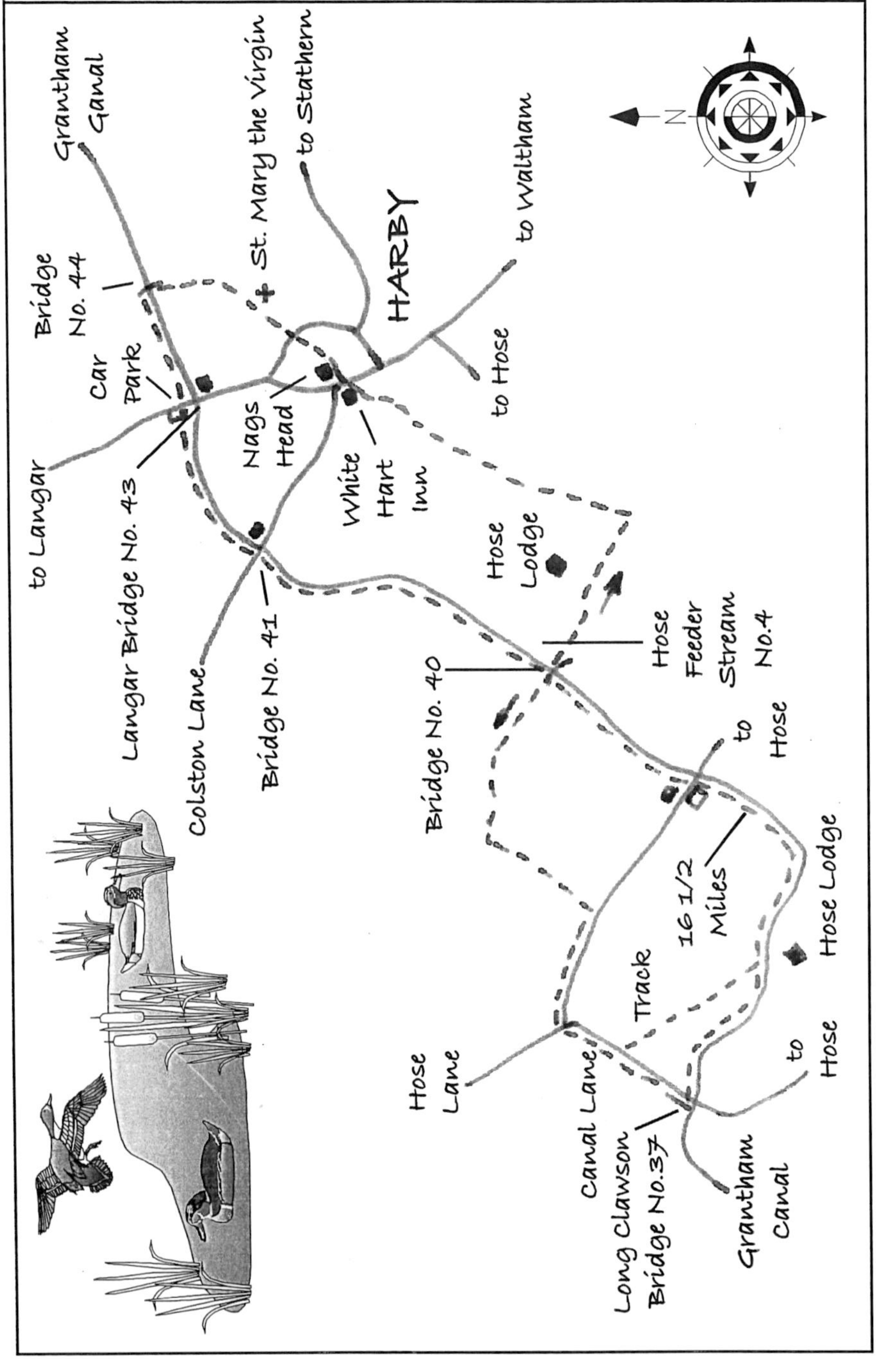

Grantham Canal

to Statheru

to Waltham

St. Mary the Virgin

HARBY

Bridge No. 44

Car Park

to Hose

Nags Head

White Hart Inn

to Langar

Langar Bridge No. 43

Colston Lane

Bridge No. 41

Hose Lodge

Hose Feeder Stream No.4

Bridge No. 40

to Hose

16 1/2 Miles

Hose Lodge

Track

Hose Lane

Canal Lane

Long Clawson Bridge No.37

Grantham Canal

to Hose

HARBY
- 7 MILES
- allow 3 hours

Basic route - Langar Bridge No. 43 - Grantham Canal - Bridge No. 40 - Meadows Lane - Canal Lane - Long Clawson Bridge No. 37 - Grantham Canal - Bridge No. 40 - Harby - St. Mary the Virgin church, Harby - Bridge No. 44 - Grantham Canal - Langar Bridge.

Map - O.S. 1:25,000 Explorer Series No. 260 - Nottingham & the Vale of Belvoir.

Car park and start - Langar Bridge No. 43, beside the canal on Langar lane - Langar - Harby road. Grid Ref. 744316.

Inns - White Hart and Nag's Head in Harby.

ABOUT THE WALK - A figure of eight walk exploring approximately 3 miles of canal, just inside Leicestershire. You pass the 16 1/2 miles from the Trent, canal milepost; the halfway point of the canal between Nottingham and Grantham. Near the end of the walk you walk through Harby, passed two inns and St. Mary's church before regaining the canal for the final 1/4 mile back to the start at Langar Bridge. The canal is a mixture of water and reed and is full of wildlife, as you walk through a quiet area of countryside. Some of the paths are little used but are all well stiled and signed. Harby has a small creamery where Stilton Cheese is made.

53

WALKING INSTRUCTIONS - Starting from Langar Bridge gain the canal and turn right, with the Harby Maintenance Yard (British Waterways), opposite. Follow the canal southwards, with canal on your left. Pass canal milepost - 18 1/4 miles from the Trent. In 1/4 mile reach Bridge No. 41 - Colston Lane - and pass Harby Wharf on your left. Continue beside the water filled canal for nearly another mile to Bridge No. 40 - a cement bridge; this is the crossover point of the figure of eight. You will cross the bridge later. First turn right onto a track - a bridlepath - and follow it with a hedge on your right for 1/4 mile to a circular water trough. Turn half left, guided by bridlepath signs and yellow topped posts. At the next post turn left along the edge of the field to a small gate and yellow post. Turn right then left to continue along the lefthand side of the field, along a track, to Meadows Lane. Turn right and in 1/4 mile at the road junction, turn left along Canal Lane. In 100 yards you can, as bridlepath signed, turn left and follow a track back to the canal, or keep ahead along the lane to Long Clawson Bridge No. 37. In both cases turn left to continue beside the canal on your right.

In 1/4 mile at Marriots Bridge No. 38, to your left is the track from Canal Lane and on the otherside of the canal, Hose Lodge. Continue beside the canal, now water filled, and in 1/4 mile pass the 16 1/2 mile canal post - the canal's halfway point. Continue to Bridge 39, with a car park. Follow the canal for more than 1/4 mile to Bridge No. 40. On the other side of the bridge is the marked canal - Hose Feeder Stream No. 4. Turn right across the bridge to a gate. Keep straight ahead with the hedge on your left to another gate. Continue with the hedge on your left to a stile and footbridge. Cross and now continue with the hedge on your right to a gate and track from another Hose Lodge. Once into the next field turn left, keeping to the lefthand side of the field to a stile in the far lefthand corner. Continue with the hedge on your left to the next stile. Keep ahead to the next then left across the field corner to the next one. Cross the field to the far middle corner and a stile. Continue with the hedge on your left to a footbridge on your left. Cross and bear slightly right to the next stile and onto the next one a short distance ahead. Follow the fenced path left then right to gain the road in Harby; to your left is the White Hart Inn and Nags Head Inn.

Cross the road and continue ahead past the Methodist Chapel on your left and Wagoners Lodge on your right, soon onto a tarmaced path to a path junction. Turn right then left into Watson's lane. Follow it to the main road and War Memorial Cross. Go straight across, signed St. Mary the Virgin Church. Continue to the church gate and turn left then right along the field edge to a stile. Follow the defined path leftwards across the field before turning left to a concrete bridge No. 44 and cross to the towpath. Turn left keeping the canal on your left and in 1/4 mile regain Langar Lane and car park on your right.

St. Mary's church. Harby.

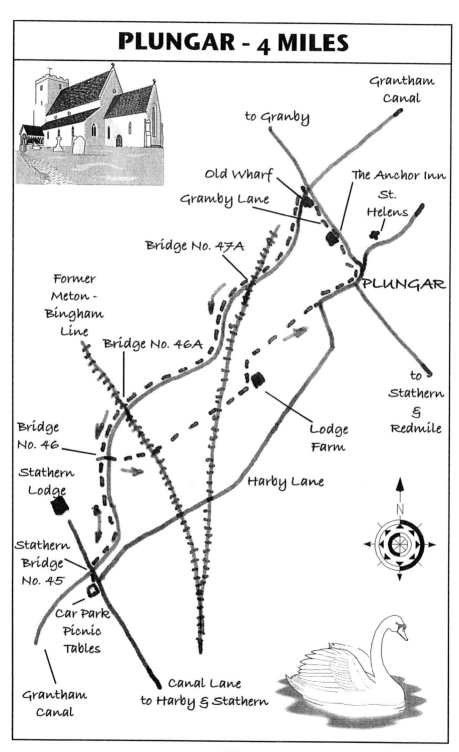

PLUNGAR - 4 MILES

Grantham
Canal

to Granby

Old Wharf

Gramby Lane

The Anchor Inn

St.
Helens

PLUNGAR

Bridge No. 47A

Former
Meton -
Bingham
Line

Bridge No. 46A

Bridge
No. 46

Stathern
Lodge

Lodge
Farm

to
Stathern
&
Redmile

Harby Lane

N

Stathern
Bridge
No. 45

Car Park
Picnic
Tables

Canal Lane
to Harby & Stathern

Grantham
Canal

PLUNGAR
- 4 MILES
- allow 1 1/2 hours.

Basic route - Stathern Bridge (No. 45) - Grantham Canal - Bridge No. 46 - Lodge Farm - Plungar - Old Wharf - Grantham Canal - Stathern Bridge.

Map - O.S. 1:25,000 Explorer Series No. 260 - Nottingham & the Vale of Belvoir.

Car Park and start - Stathern Bridge No. 45, with picnic tables. One mile north of the Harby-Stathern road, on Canal Road - signed To Dove Cottage, beside the canal at Grid Ref. 756324. Canal Lane becomes Harby Lane, and is the lane to Plungar.

Inn - The aptly named, Anchor Inn in Plungar.

ABOUT THE WALK - A short but interesting walk along the canal, crossing two former railways, before reaching the village of Plungar. Just off the route is St. Helen's church. A short road walk brings you to the Old Wharf buildings and the canal. You follow the canal all the way back to Stathern Bridge, no doubt seeing swans, coots, moorhens and mallards. In the spring their nests and young can be seen on the opposite bank. The whole of this walk is in Leicestershire.

WALKING INSTRUCTIONS - Cross the bridge and turn left to the towpath and left again to walk under the bridge. Continue with the towpath on your right; the canal is water filled with reeds. In more than 1/4 mile reach Bridge No. 46, turn right across the bridge and walk past trees to a railway bridge. Cross over the former railway line - the Melton - Bingham line built in 1879. Continue ahead with a hedge on your right and as you near the next railway bridge bear slightly left to a stile and cross another former line to a stile on the left. Keep to the righthand side of the field, following it left by a hedge to near Lodge Farm and another stile. Turn left to the next stile and then down to the righthand corner of the field to a gate. Continue with a hedge on your left - the field on the right has some good examples of ridge and furrow ploughing (medieval). At the end of the field gain a stile and Harby Lane. Keep straight ahead into the village and soon following Barkestone Lane. Turn left along Granby Lane; ahead on Barkestone Lane is St. Helen's church.

Pass the Anchor Inn on Granby Lane and soon afterwards pas the Old Wharf buildings beside the canal. Turn left to the towpath and follow the canal on your left for the next 1 1/2 miles back to Stathern Bridge. Pass bridge No. 48 and canal milepost - 20 1/4 miles from the Trent. Pass the first railway bridge No. 47A and 1/2 mile later No. 46A, the former Melton - Bingham line. Continue ahead and soon pass bridge No. 46 where you crossed the canal earlier and more than 1/4 mile later regain Stathern Bridge and small car park. Beside the bridge can be seen a canal turning circle.

Bridge No. 45 - Stathern Bridge.

ST. HELEN'S CHURCH, PLUNGAR - The church is believed to date back to 1240 and has some interesting items believed to have come from Croxden Abbey(Leicestershire), when it was dissolved in 1538. Two animal carvings in the stalls are said to have come from there. On the exterior tower wall can be seen three eroded carvings of one of the stories of Reynard, a fox. St. Helen was a Queen and Pilgrim who died in 328 AD?

PLUNGAR, REDMILE AND BARKESTONE-LE-VALE - 5 MILES

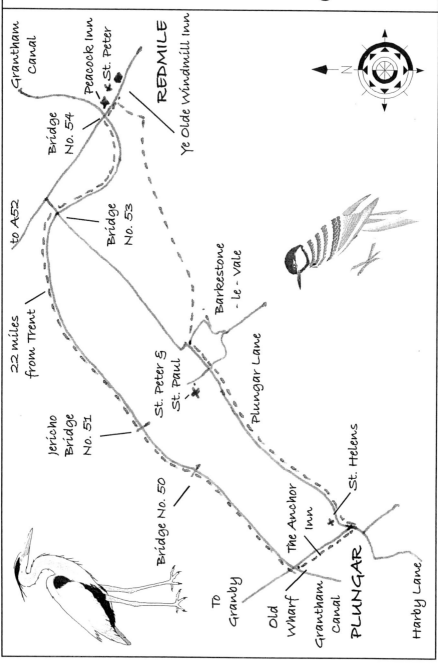

Grantham Canal

Peacock Inn

St. Peter

REDMILE

Ye Olde Windmill Inn

Bridge No. 54

to A52

Bridge No. 53

Barkestone - le - vale

22 miles from Trent

St. Peter & St. Paul

Plungar Lane

Jericho Bridge No. 51

St. Helens

Bridge No. 50

The Anchor Inn

To Granby

Old Wharf

Grantham Canal

PLUNGAR

Harby Lane

PLUNGAR, REDMILE AND BARKESTONE - LE - VALE - 5 MILES - allow 2 1/2 hours.

Basic Route - Plungar - Grantham Canal - Jericho Bridge No. 51 - Bridge No. 54 - Redmile - Barkestone - Le - Vale - Plungar.

O.S. MAP

Map - O.S. 1:25,000 Explorer Series No. 260 - Nottingham & Vale of Belvoir.

VISITOR PARKING

Car Park and start - Roadside in Plungar, on Granby Lane, near canal. Alternative, roadside in Redmile.

Inns - The Anchor Inn, Plungar. The Peacock Inn and Ye Olde Windmill Inn, Redmile.

ABOUT THE WALK - First you follow more than two miles of the canal, which is a mixture of water and reed. This section of the canal is very quiet and includes some really attractive unspoilt sections. Swans and Canada Geese were nesting on the canal and in the reeds I watched a reed warbler singing its heart out. Redmile has an interesting church and two inns, before you cross the fields to Barkestone - le - Vale. Southwards the towers of Belvoir Castle dominate the wooded slopes. Barkestone - le - Vale is a delightful unspoilt village with a more modern church, but no inn. A short walk along Plungar Lane returns you to Plungar at its church, dedicated to St. Helens, and back past The Anchor Inn to your start. The whole walk is in Leicestershire.

61

WALKING INSTRUCTIONS - From Granby Lane in Plungar, head northwards past the Old Wharf building on your left to the canal and bridge No. 49. Turn right onto the canal and keep the canal on your righthand side for the next 2 1/2 miles (50 mins). Soon pass milepost - 20 1/2 miles from Trent. More than a mile later pass Jericho Bridge No. 51 with the spire of St. Peter and St. Paul church in Barkestone - le - Vale to your right. You will be passing there in another hour. Continue beside the canal along a delightful section, passing the 22 mile post and onto Bridge No. 53. Continue for another 1/2 mile to Bridge No. 54 and Redmile. Turn right into the village, with the Peacock Inn on your left. Just after is the church, dedicated to St. Peter.

Turn right into Church Lane and follow it past the houses, following it left then right to a path sign close to the concrete drive to the sewage works. Walk a few yards along the drive and bear right in a defined path to a stile and yellow topped post. Gently ascend the next field passing a solitary path marker post and onto the top righthand corner of the field and a stile. Continue diagonally across the next field; the spire of Barkestone - le - Vale church acts as a rough guide, although your path line is well to the left of it. Reach a stile and footbridge and go straight across the next field to another stile and footbridge. Over bear half right to the next stile and then across the field to the far righthand corner to a gate before the houses and Fishpond Lane. Turn right and in a few yards left along New Causeway, past the houses of Barkestone - le - Vale. At the crossroads, to your right is The Green which leads to the church and on along to Jericho Bridge.

Keep straight ahead, as signed - Plungar, walking along Plungar Lane, to the village more than 1/2 mile away. Pass St. Helen's church and turn right down Granby Lane. Pass The Anchor Inn and soon regain the parking area close to the canal where you began.

Bridge No. 50, with rope grooves.

The canal near Redmile.

ST. PETER'S CHURCH, REDMILE - Dates back to the 12th. century. A Saxon coffin lid can be seen behind the pulpit, which was found in the 1870's. The tower is 150 ft high. Many of the local gravestones have the "Belvoir Angel", carved on them.

EQUIPMENT NOTES

Today there is a bewildering variety of walking gear, much is superfluous to general walking in Britain. As a basic observation, people over dress for the outdoors. Basically equipment should be serviceable and do the task. I don't use walking poles; humans were built to walk with two legs! The following are some of my thoughts gathered from my walking experiences.

BOOTS - For summer use and day walking I wear lightweight boots. For high mountains and longer trips I prefer a good quality boot with a full leather upper, of medium weight, traditional style ,with a vibram sole. I always add a foam cushioned insole to help cushion the base of my feet.

SOCKS - I generally wear two thick pairs as this helps minimise blisters. The inner pair are of loop stitch variety and approximately 80% wool. The outer are also a thick pair of approximately 80% wool. I often wear double inner socks, which minimise blisters.

CLOTHES & WATERPROOFS - for general walking I wear a T shirt or cotton shirt with a cotton wind jacket on top, and shorts - even in snow! You generate heat as you walk and I prefer to layer my clothes to avoid getting too hot. Depending on the season will dictate how many layers you wear. In soft rain I just use my wind jacket for I know it quickly dries out. In heavy or consistent rain I slip on a poncho, which covers me and my pack and allows air to circulate, while keeping me dry. Only in extreme conditions will I don over-trousers, much preferring to get wet and feel comfortable. I never wear gaiters, except when cross country skiing, or in snow and glacier crossings. I find running shorts and sleeveless T shirts ideal for summer.

FOOD - as I walk I carry bars of chocolate, for they provide instant energy and are light to carry. In winter a flask of hot coffee is welcome. I never carry water and find no hardship from not doing so, but this is a personal matter! From experience I find the more I drink the more I want and sweat. You should always carry some extra food such as trail mix & candy bars etc., for emergencies. Full milk is a very underestimated source of food and liquid.

RUCKSACKS - for day walking I use a rucksack of about 30/40 litre capacity and although it leaves excess space it does mean that the sac is well padded, with an internal frame and padded shoulder straps, chest strap and waist strap. Inside apart from the basics for one day, in winter I carry gloves, wear a hat/cap and carry a spare pullover and a pair of socks.

MAP & COMPASS - when I am walking I always have the relevant map - preferably 1:25,000 scale - open in my hand. This enables me to constantly check that I am walking the right way. In case of bad weather I carry a compass, which once mastered gives you complete confidence in thick cloud or mist - you should always know where you are; I have a built in direction finder! Map reading and compass work is a skill and should be learnt. With modern technology you can now downloaded OS maps to your phone, record your walk, mileage, calories, steps taken, walking speed and time taken.

REDMILE AND MUSTON GORSE
BRIDGE No. 57 - 5 MILES

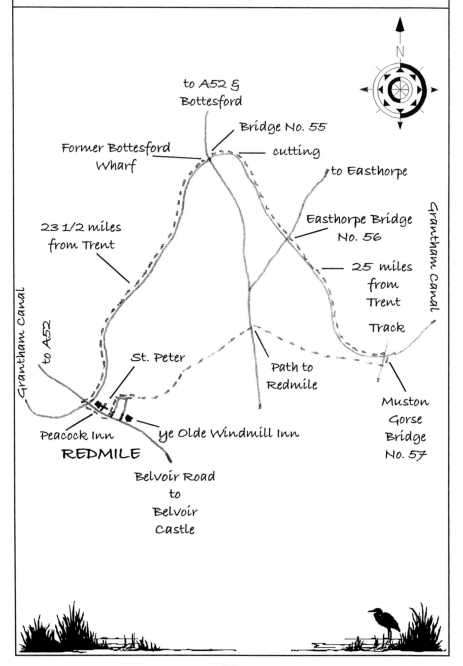

to A52 &
Bottesford

Bridge No. 55

Former Bottesford
Wharf

cutting

to Easthorpe

Easthorpe Bridge
No. 56

23 1/2 miles
from Trent

25 miles
from
Trent

Track

Grantham Canal

St. Peter

Path to
Redmile

Muston
Gorse
Bridge
No. 57

to A52

Peacock Inn

ye Olde Windmill Inn

REDMILE

Belvoir Road
to
Belvoir
Castle

REDMILE AND MUSTON GORSE BRIDGE No. 57
- 5 MILES
- allow 2 1/2 miles.

Basic route - Redmile - Grantham Canal - Site of Bottesford Wharf - Bridge No. 55 - Bridge No. 56 - Muston Gorse Bridge No. 57 - Bottesford Road - Redmile.

Map - O.S. 1:25,000 Explorer Series No. 260 - Nottingham & Vale of Belvoir.

Car park and start - Roadside parking in Redmile.

Inns - The Peacock Inn and Ye Olde Windmill Inn, Redmile.

ABOUT THE WALK - The canal at Redmile does a three mile loop northwards towards Bottesford, maintaining its level route before the locks at Woolsthorpe and the final climb to Grantham. This is quietest section of the canal, passing the site of Bottesford Wharf and through a shallow cutting. You leave the canal at Muston Gorse Bridge No. 57 and cross the fields eastwards back to Redmile. Here is an interesting church and a couple of inns. The route can be added to the Plungar walk making a ten mile circular walk.

WALKING INSTRUCTIONS - Walk along the road past St. Peter's church and Peacock Inn - the Peacock is a symbol of the Dukes of Rutland - and reach bridge No. 54 and the canal. Turn right onto the towpath.

Walk beside the canal on your right and soon pass a former turning circle for the narrow boats on your right. Keep beside the canal for the next couple of miles. Pass 23 1/2 mile post, then 24 miles before Bridge No. 55 and the site of the Bottesford Wharf. The canal now passes through a delightful shallow cutting and more than 1/2 mile later gain Easthorpe Bridge, No. 56 and a seat. Continue by the canal passing the 25 mile post and nearly 3/4 mile later (15 mins), gain the track and bridge No. 57, near Muston Gorse Farm.

Turn right across the canal and a few yards later right at the footpath sign, showing the sole of a shoe; a typical Leicestershire path sign - a horseshoe is used as the symbol for a bridleway. The path is defined and leads near the canal at first before bearing left to a solitary oak tree and a footbridge, beside a yellow topped post. Continue to another footbridge and then across a large field to a path sign and the Belvoir Road from Bottesford. Go straight across to the path sign - Redmile. Go diagonally across the large field to a yellow topped post. Turn right to a track and turn left along it. Follow it with a hedge on your right as it curves right to the houses of Redmile and Drift Hill. Keep ahead on the lane taking the second lane on your left - Bakers Lane, into the village centre. You can soon, alternatively, turn right on a path which brings you to the play area close to the church. But by keeping on the lane to the main road in the village, you turn right and pass the former Bake House, before passing the play area and church. Just ahead is the Peacock Inn, close to where you began.

The peaceful canal near the former Bottesford Wharf.

Muston Cross.

WOOLSTHORPE AND MUSTON
- 8 MILES

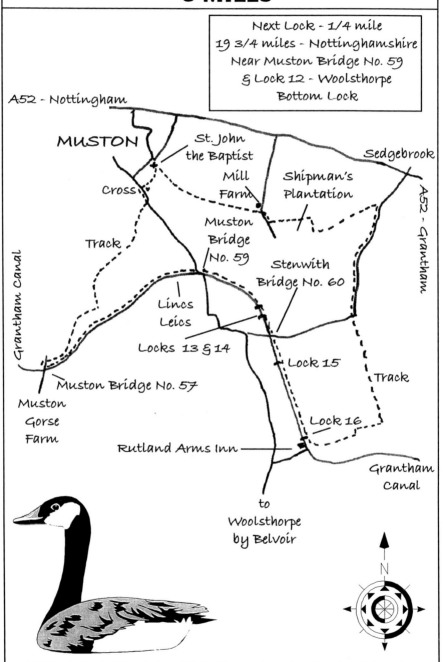

Next Lock - 1/4 mile
19 3/4 miles - Nottinghamshire
Near Muston Bridge No. 59
& Lock 12 - Woolsthorpe
Bottom Lock

A52 - Nottingham

MUSTON

St. John
the Baptist

Sedgebrook

Mill
Farm

Shipman's
Plantation

Cross

A52 - Grantham

Track

Muston
Bridge
No. 59

Stenwith
Bridge No. 60

Grantham Canal

Lincs
Leics

Locks 13 & 14

Lock 15

Muston Bridge No. 57

Track

Muston
Gorse
Farm

Lock 16

Rutland Arms Inn

Grantham
Canal

to
Woolsthorpe
by Belvoir

N

WOOLSTHORPE AND MUSTON
- 8 MILES
- allow 3 1/2 hours.

Basic route - Woolsthorpe Wharf - Grantham Canal - Locks 16 to 12 - Muston Gorse Bridge No. 57 - Muston Cross - Muston Church - Mill Farm - Sewstern Lane - Shipman's Plantation - Woolsthorpe Lane - Longmoor Lane (Track) - Woolsthorpe Wharf.

O.S. MAP

Map - O.S. 1:25,000 Explorer Series No. 247 - Grantham, Bottesford & Colsterworth.

VISITOR PARKING

Car park and start - limited roadside parking at Woolsthorpe Wharf, near the Rutland Arms Inn.

Inns - Rutland Arms Inn, Woolsthorpe Wharf.

ABOUT THE WALK - First you walk beside the canal past a restored lock before passing several abandoned ones. You pass several bridges, one of whom - Bridge No. 59 - Muston Bridge - has examples of rope grooves from when the narrow boats were pulled along by horses. Just after is the notice that the next lock is 19 3/4 miles away in Nottinghamshire. This 20 mile pound - the section between locks - is one of the longest on any canal. A short distance later you step into Leicestershire - you started in Lincolnshire! A mile later you gain Muston Gorse Bridge No. 57. Here you leave the canal and follow a track to Muston, passing its fine cross and onto its church, dedicated to St. John the Baptist. A good path leads eastwards across the fields to Mill Farm and the Viking Way, which you followed at the start. A short distance along it you continue eastwards to Woolsthorpe Lane. Here you head southwards before turning right along a track back to Woolsthrope Wharf where you began. To the south on the wooded slopes can be seen Belvoir Castle.

WALKING INSTRUCTIONS - Continue past the Rutland Arms Inn and gain the canal. Turn left along it, keeping it on your left. Pass the restored Lock No. 16. More than 1/2 mile later reach the ruined lock No. 15. Here the Viking Way leaves the canal side. Keep ahead by the canal to pass Stenwith Bridge No. 60. Continue past the ruined locks No. 14 and 13 and onto Woolsthrope Bottom Lock No. 12. Just after pass Muston Bridge No. 59, with visible rope grooves. Continue by the canal for a further mile, stepping into Leicestershire. Pass Bridge No. 58 - Longmoor Bridge, then canal milepost - 26 miles from Trent, and ten minutes later Muston Gorse Bridge No. 57; you will soon be in Nottinghamshire, briefly!

Leave the canal here and turn right on the track. In a few yards, as Byway signed turn right and walk around the field edge with the canal just over the hedge. In 300 yards the track bears left away from the canal and is well defined and marked with yellow posts with red arrows. The track swings left then right and becomes a hedged track and more than a mile from the canal gains Woolsthorpe Lane. Turn left and soon pass Muston Cross and seat on the right. Immediately afterwards, turn right as path signed, along The Green. Keep straight ahead between the houses on the tarmaced path down to a footbridge. Over, turn left towards the church, dedicated to St. John the Baptist, reached by a stile on the left. At it, turn right to walk beside the hedge on your left to a stile and trees. The other side bear right to walk along the righthand edge of the field, keeping a stream on your right. In 1/4 mile keep straight ahead, now on a track to Mill Farm, Sewstern Lane and Viking Way. Turn right passing the house on your right and in 150 yards approach Shipman's Plantation. Just before it turn left, as path signed, to a footbridge, and leave the Viking Way. Continue with the plantation on your right, and where it turns right, follow its edge to a hedge. Bear left and keep the hedge on your right towards a farm and Woolsthrope Lane (another one). Just before the farm turn right, as signed, through a gate gap and walk along the lefthand corner of the field to a stile and gain Woolsthorpe lane.

Turn right and follow the lane southwards for little over 1/2 mile. Just after Long Meadow House on your left, the lane turns sharp right. Keep straight ahead, now on a hedged track - Longmoor Lane - and in almost

3/4 mile turn right onto the first hedged track on your right. Ahead where you turn can be seen Longmoor Bridge over the canal. Follow the track for 1/2 mile back to the canal and the Rutland Arms Inn. Cross Bridge No. 61 and regain your start.

MUSTON CROSS - A fine cross with steps. The four corners of the cross base have a shield. Just beyond the church, dedicated to St. John the Baptist, is a particularly attractive thatched cottage.

Rutland Arms Inn and restored lock No. 16.

Lock No. 15.

Stenwith Bridge No. 60.

Next lock 19 3/4 miles!

Leicestershire/Lincolnshire boundary canal marker.

WOOLSTHORPE by BELVOIR AND DENTON RESERVOIR - 8 MILES

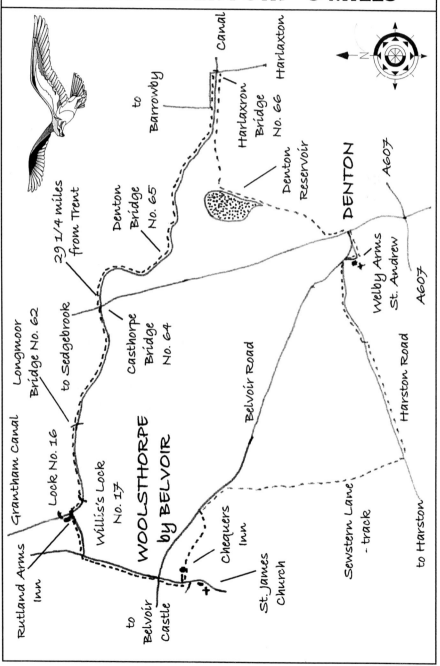

Canal

to Barrowby

Harlaxton Bridge No. 66

Harlaxton

Denton Bridge No. 65

29 1/4 miles from Trent

Denton Reservoir

DENTON

A607

Welby Arms
St. Andrew

A607

Longmoor Bridge No. 62

to Sedgebrook

Casthorpe Bridge No. 64

Belvoir Road

Harston Road

Grantham Canal

Lock No. 16

Willis's Lock No. 17

WOOLSTHORPE by BELVOIR

Chequers Inn

St. James Church

Sewstern Lane - track

to Harston

Rutland Arms Inn

to Belvoir Castle

WOOLSTHORPE by BELVOIR AND DENTON
- 8 MILES
- allow 3 hours.

Basic route - Woolsthorpe by Belvoir - Woolsthrope Wharf- Grantham Canal - Harlaxton Bridge - Denton Reservoir - Denton - Harston Road - Sewstern Lane - Fanny's Wood - Woolsthrope by Belvoir.

Map - O.S. 1:25,000 Explorer Series No. 247 - Grantham.

Car Park and start - roadside parking in Main Street, Woolsthorpe by Belvoir. Small parking area at Harlaxton Bridge. Roadside parking at Casthorpe Bridge No. 64 - Denton Lane.

Inns - Rutland Arms Inn, Woolsthorpe Wharf. Welby Arms, Denton. The Chequer's Inn, Woolsthorpe by Belvoir.

ABOUT THE WALK - From Woolsthrope by Belvoir you soon reach the canal at Woolsthrope Wharf and the final locks of the canal. You follow the canal for three miles through lovely and unspoilt countryside to Harlaxton Bridge No. 66. Here you cross to the otherside of the canal and walk back near it before crossing fields to gain the stunningly peaceful Denton Reservoir. Here coots, Canada Geese and Grebe can be seen. Paths lead you Denton and its attractive village and church. From here a path close to the Harston Road brings you to Sewstern Lane; part of the Viking Way, the track is lined with sweet chestnut trees. The final section of the route you descend to the Chequers Inn in Woolsthorpe by Belvoir, with views to Belvoir Castle, the home of the Dukes of Rutland.

WALKING INSTRUCTIONS - Starting from Main Street in Woolsthorpe by Belvoir, walk northwards to the cross roads and road to Belvoir Castle. Go straight across and follow the pavement on the lefthand side of the road - Sedgebrook Road. In 1/2 mile turn right along the drive to the Rutland Arms Inn and canal. Cross the bridge - No. 61 - and turn right to gain the towpath. Pass Willis's Lock No. 17 and Woolsthorpe Top Lock No. 18, the last one on the canal. Grantham is now 5 miles away. Continue beside the canal on your right for the next 3 miles (one hour). Pass Longmoor Bridge No. 62 with visible rope grooves in the white corner stones. Pass Bridle Bridge No. 63 and Casthorpe Bridge No. 64. Then Denton Bridge No. 65 and wharf, after the 29 3/4 miles from Trent milepost. Pass a turning circle on the right and 3/4 mile later Harlaxton Bridge No. 66. Here leave the canal by turning left and crossing the bridge.

On the otherside, as path signed - Denton Reservoir - ascend steps and follow the path on the righthand side, with the canal on your right. In more than 1/4 mile reach a stile - not the one on the left, and keep straight ahead with the hedge on your left. Reach a stile and footbridge in the corner and continue ahead, the path soon becomes a track then a path again as you cross a footbridge and ascend steps to reach Denton Reservoir. Turn left and walk beside the reservoir and in 1/4 mile cross a footbridge and turn left, leaving the reservoir, to walk along a path with a stream on your left to three stiles before a stile and path and the Casthorpe Road. Turn left and soon right along Church Street. Where it turns right keep ahead to reach the Welby Arms and lane on the right, which you will take next. But first it is worth visiting the church ahead and see a delightful house opposite. Turn right down the lane to the Belvoir Road to Woolsthorpe by Belvoir. Turn left and left again in a few yards onto the Harston Road.

Pass Denton Manor Estate Office drive on your left and once past its perimeter walls and gateway, on your left is a stile and path. This keeps you off the road along the righthand edge of the fields and in more than 1/2 mile returns you back to the road at a crossroads. Turn right and cross Harston Road and keep ahead along Sewstern Lane. This is part of the Viking Way whose symbol is a viking helmet. Pass New Cottages on the left and the lane now becomes a hedged track lined with horse chestnuts. Follow the track for a mile to the Belvoir Road. Turn left and in less than

1/4 mile at the top of the hill, turn left, as path signed onto a track through woodland. Near its edge go through a stile and turn right and keeping the wood on the right and soon start descending, with views ahead to Belvoir Castle. Descend to a stile and cricket field. Walk along its lefthand edge to the Chequers Inn and on down to the Main Road in Woolsthrope by Belvoir, where you began.

Willis Lock, No. 17.

Denton Reservoir.

The perfectly proportined house opposite Denton Church.

ST. ANDREW'S CHURCH, DENTON - Inside are several impressive monuments to former lords of the manor. These include Johannes Blyth and family, dated 1602. A standing white alabaster monument to Richard Welby of Denton, dated 1714, recalls his illustrious life.

ST. JAMES CHURCH, WOOLSTHROPE by BELVOIR - The earlier church burnt down during the Civil War. The present church was built in 1847 at a cost £3,500. St. James is the patron saint of Spain and many pilgrims routes lead to his shrine at Santiago de Compostela in Northern Spain. His symbol is a staff, satchel and shell and a stained glass window near the font depicts him - St. Jacobus. The seventh Duke of Rutland who died August 4th. 1906, has a plaque here. Most of the Dukes are buried and have large monuments in Bottesford church.

HARLAXTON AND GRANTHAM
- 7 MILES

GRANTHAM

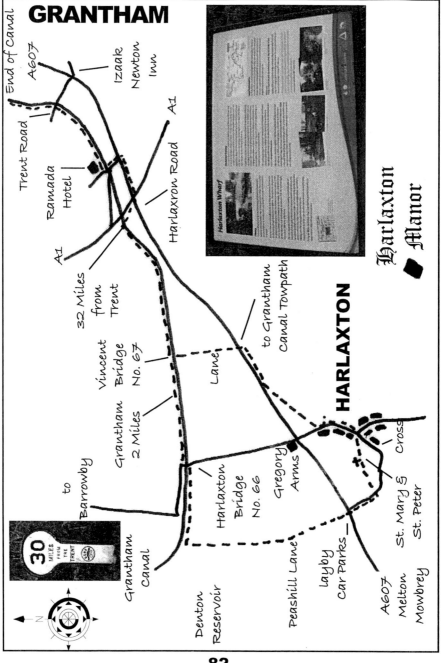

End of Canal

A607

Izaak Newton Inn

Trent Road

A1

Ramada Hotel

Harlaxton Road

A1

Harlaxton Manor

32 Miles from Trent

to Grantham Canal Towpath

Vincent Bridge No. 67

Lane

HARLAXTON

Grantham 2 Miles

to Barrowby

Harlaxton Bridge No. 66

Gregory Arms

Cross

St. Mary & St. Peter

Grantham Canal

Denton Reservoir

Peashill Lane

Layby Car Parks

A607 Melton Mowbrey

30 MILES FROM THE TRENT

N

HARLAXTON
AND GRANTHAM
- 7 MILES
- allow 3 hours.

Basic route - A607, Harlaxton - Peashill Lane - Grantham Canal - Harlaxton Bridge - Vincent Bridge No. 67 - A1 bridge - Ramada Hotel - Trent Road - A1 bridge - Vincent Bridge No. 67 - Harlaxton Road - Harlaxton - A607.

Map - O.S. 1:25,000 Explorer Series No. 247 - Grantham.

Car Park and start - Lay-by's on either side of the A607 on the western side of Harlaxton village. Close to Rectory lane into the village and Peashill Lane, your start out path. Grid Ref. 878326. Alternative parking - limited roadside parking in Harlaxton village; small parking area at Harlaxton Bridge and roadside parking in Grantham near Trent Lane and Izaak Newton Inn.

Inns - Izaak Newton, Grantham; just off the route. Gregory Arms, Harlaxton; just off the route.

ABOUT THE WALK - The aim is to explore the final stages of the canal into Grantham. Because of the town layout you walk the final part of the canal twice. First you walk along a track and bridlepath to the canal and follow it past Harlaxton Bridge to the appropriately named Trent Lane in Grantham. You return back along the canal to Vincent Bridge and walk along a lane and path to gain the most attractive village of Harlaxton and views to Harlaxton Manor. You pass the church before regaining the A607 road.

83

WALKING INSTRUCTIONS - Starting from the lay-by car park beside the A607 on the western side of Harlaxton, turn left along Peashill Lane, bridlepath signed and lane to Village Farm. Opposite is Rectory Lane your return route. Keep straight ahead along the lane and in more than 1/4 mile where it turns left for Village Farm, keep ahead through a gate and continue with the hedge on your left along a track and in more than 1/4 mile reach a stile and path beyond with the canal ahead. Turn right along the path, keeping the canal on your left to the Harlaxton road and Harlaxton Bridge No. 66 & Harlaxton Wharf on your left. Cross the bridge over the canal and turn right onto the towpath; Grantham is 2 1/2 miles away. Keep the canal on your right and pass the stone mile post - Grantham 2 miles. Less than 1/4 mile later pass Vincent Bridge no. 67, this is where you will leave the canal on your return from Grantham.

First, continue beside the canal and in 1/2 mile near the A1 Grantham bypass and the end of the canal beside canal milepost - 32 miles from Trent. There is still a mile of canal left to explore. Turn right along the path below the A1 to the Harlaxton Road. Turn left and pass under the A1. The actual canal is to your left behind the Squash Club. Continue along the road and turn left at the first road, signed Hotel & Spa (Ramada) and A1. A short distance along here and before the hotel, turn right and regain the canal towpath. Follow it to Trent Road and on to its end. Turn round and retrace your steps back to the Ramada Hotel and along Harlaxton Road and under the A1. Turn right and regain the canal. Follow it more than 1/2 mile to Vincent Bridge No. 67. Cross the bridge to your left and follow the lane to the A607 road, with a sign - To Grantham Canal Towpath.

Turn right along the pavement on the lefthand side of the road. In less than 1/4 mile on your left is a stile and footpath sign. Follow the defined path across the field and cross the drive to Harlaxton Manor; the impressive manor, now a college (Evansville University of Indiana), is to your left. Continue on the path to a stile and kissing gate and High Street, Harlaxton. To your right is the Gregory Arms; the Gregory family originally owned Harlaxton Manor. Turn left and in a short distance turn right along Trotters Lane. Just beyond it is a cross and the delightful Coneygreave House. At the top of Trotter lane, turn left to walk through the churchyard of St. Mary's and St. Peter's church. Continue past the porch to a gate. Keep the hedge on your left to two gates and onto Rectory Lane. Turn right to regain the A607.

The canal near Vincent Bridge.

Stone canal milepost - 2 miles from Grantham.

The final canal milepost before the A1 bypass in Grantham.

The final section of the canal near the Ramada Hotel.

The Cross and Coneygreave House, Harlaxton.

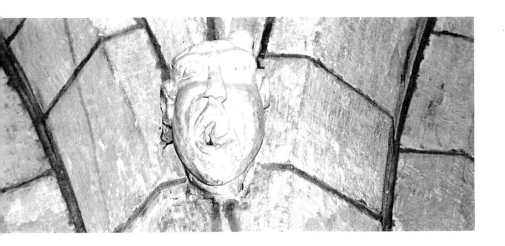

ST. MARY & ST. PETER CHURCH, HARLAXTON - For a small village this is an extremely fine building dating back to the 12th. century. Inside is a 600 year old font, Lady's Chapel and Trinity Chapel. There are monuments to the Gregory family and several interesting carved faces and angels.

GRANTHAM CANAL - END TO END WALK - 33 MILES

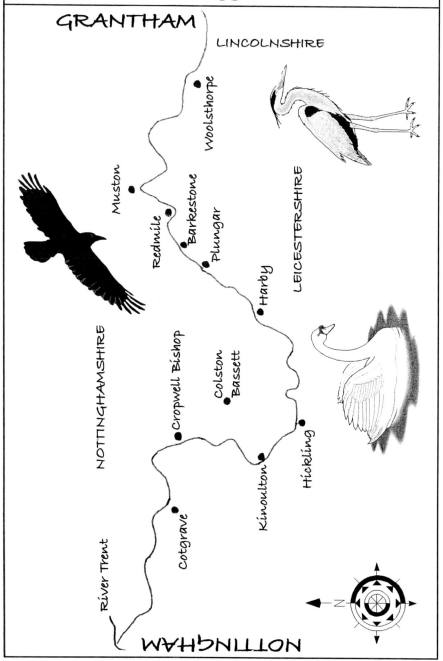

GRANTHAM

LINCOLNSHIRE

Woolsthorpe

Muston

Redmile

Barkestone

Plungar

Harby

LEICESTERSHIRE

NOTTINGHAMSHIRE

Cropwell Bishop

Colston Bassett

Hickling

Kinoulton

Cotgrave

River Trent

NOTTINGHAM

GRANTHAM CANAL -
END TO END
- 33 MILES
- approximately
12, hours of walking.

Basic Route - Grantham - Woolsthorpe - Redmile - Plungar - Harby - Hickling - Kinoulton - Cotgrave - River Trent, Nottingham.

O.S. MAP

Maps - O.S. 1:25,000 Explorer Series Nos -
- 247 - Grantham, Bottesford & Colsterworth
- 260 - Nottingham & Vale of Belvoir

VISITOR PARKING

Car Parks - numerous beside the canal - see individual walks for details.

Inns - Rutland Arms Inn, Woolsthorpe Wharf. The Peacock Inn & Ye Olde Windmill Inn, Redmile. The Anchor Inn, Plungar. Plough Inn, Hickling. Lime Kiln Inn near Cropwell Wharf. Several in Nottingham at the end!

ABOUT THE WALK - I have chosen to walk the canal end to end from Grantham, for two simple reasons. Firstly, Grantham is an interesting and historic market town and worth exploring. The canal start at Trent Lane, Grantham a mile from centre, is just the canal; whereas at its end in Nottingham you come to the lock before the River Trent in a pleasant location. Secondly, all the canal mileposts - nearly every 1/4 mile - give you the distance from the Trent and how much you have left to walk! Being flat you can walk it as a challenge in a day - about 12 hours of walking. Alternatively take two days over it breaking the route at Harby - 15 miles, leaving 18 to go. Alternatively carrying on the Hickling - 20 miles and 13 to go! The only overnight camping is at Kinoulton after 21 miles. Camping is also available at the Rutland Arms Inn, Woolsthorpe Wharf, after 5 miles, leaving 28 to go! Limited overnight accommodation can be found in some of the nearby villages; check with either Grantham or Nottingham Tourist Offices for details.

WALKING INSTRUCTIONS - Rather than describe the route fully, the individual walks and maps detail the canal sections and all interlock. The following is a brief overview.

Starting from Trent Lane, off the A607 on the western side of Grantham, follow the canal and road to the A1 bridge. The other side regain the canal by the first milepost - 32 miles. Pass several canal bridges with rope grooves and after four miles reach Woolsthorpe Top Lock No. 18, your first lock. Pass Woolsthrope Wharf and Rutland Arms Inn and several locks over the next two miles to Lock 12 - Woolsthorpe Bottom Lock. Closeby is a sign saying the next lock is 19 3/4 miles away; this is one of the longest canal pounds in the country. With views of Belvoir Castle the canal snakes around the countryside following the contours of the land, as you leave Lincolnshire and cross into Leicestershire. This is the most peaceful and unspoilt section of the canal. Reach Redmile after 11 miles and from here the canal is more straight - south-west - to Plungar (13 miles) and onto the road near Harby (15 miles). After a further three miles pass under Clarke's Bridge No. 32, the last true canal bridge. Beyond the hump backed bridges have been removed and are basically flat. Another mile gain Hickling and its former canal basin, with 20 miles walked.

The canal now heads northwards to Kinoulton and Cropwell Bishop and Nottinghamshire, after 25 miles, leaving 8 to go! After passing under the Fosse Bridge and the A46 the canal heads westwards through Cotgrave Country Park. At Fosse Bridge you see locks again and in Cotgrave Country Park they have been restored. Views of Nottingham appear as you head on and cross the A52 with an inn closeby. Here you reach the outskirts of the city but the canal is well defined and heads north-westerly to the River Trent and the final lock close to the Nottingham Forest Football Ground and the Brian Clough Stadium. Turn left to Trent Bridge and into Nottingham centre. You can follow the Nottingham Canal to the centre, adding on a couple more miles!

Willis Lock, near Woolsthorpe Wharf.

WALK RECORD PAGE

The River Trent and start of the Grantham Canal - 8 miles ....

Cotgrave and the Grantham Canal - 5 miles ....

Cotgrave and Cropwell Bishop - 8 miles ....

Mackley's Bridge and Owthorpe - 6 miles ....

Mackley's Bridge, Kinoulton and Colston Bassett - 6 miles ....

Hickling, Kinoulton & Colston Bassett - 7 miles ....

Colston Bassett and Long Clawson Bridge - 8 miles ....

Harby - 7 miles ....

Plungar - 4 miles ....

Plungar, Redmile and Barkestone-le-Vale - 5 miles ....

Redmile and Muston Gorse Bridge No. 57 - 5 miles ....

Woolsthorpe and Muston - 8 miles ....

Woolsthorpe by Belvoir and Denton Reservoir - 8 miles ....

Harlaxton and Grantham - 7 miles ....

End to End Walk - 33 miles ....

THE JOHN MERRILL CANAL WALK BADGE

Complete six walks in this book and get the above special
embroidered badge and special signed certificate. Badges are Blue cloth
with lettering and lock embroidered in four colours.

BADGE ORDER FORM

Date walks completed..

NAME ....

ADDRESS ....

....

Price: £6.00 each including postage, packing, VAT and signed completion
certificate. Amount enclosed (Payable to The John Merrill Foundation) ..
From: THE JOHN MERRILL FOUNDATION,
32, Holmesdale, Waltham Cross, Hertfordshire EN8 8QY
HAPPY WALKING T SHIRT - white & 4 colours - £10.00
e-mail - marathonhiker@aol.com
www.johnmerrillwalkguides.co.uk

********** *YOU MAY PHOTOCOPY THIS FORM* ***********

93

CANAL FEATURES TO LOOK FOR -

STOP PLANKS - In various places can be seen vertical grooves in the canal walls - especially near bridges - with handled planks stacked nearby. The planks are slotted into the grooves sealing the canal while repairs or cleaning of a drained section is carried out.

ROPE GROOVES - on the side of the bridges, sometimes with either cast iron or wooden shields, can be seen the grooves cut by the horse tow lines over the decades. A memory of how boats were carried along the canal.

TURNOVER/CROSSOVER BRIDGES - In a few places the towpath switches sides of the canal and a bridge was built to enable the horse to cross over without unhitching the line.

SWING BRIDGES - As the name implies, the bridge could be swung out across the canal or swung to the side to allow boats to pass.

BALANCED BRIDGES - Bridges finely balanced that can be either pushed upwards out of the way or lowered across the canal for people, tractors and cattle to cross.

SKEW BRIDGES - Most canal bridges are built at right angles to the canal. In a few cases to avoid the Z bend in the road, the bridge was built at an angle.

MILEPOSTS - Not every canal has mileposts, but there are path signs giving the mileage. The Trent and Mersey Canal has their own and distinct mileposts, showing the mileage from Shardlow and Preston Brook.. Grantham Canal has mileage from River Trent.

LOCK AND BRIDGE NUMBERS - Not every Canal/Navigation numbers them; many just rely on their name.

POUND - The length of canal between two locks.

WINDING HOLE - A small area/arm of the main canal, usually near a lock, for turning the narrowboat round.

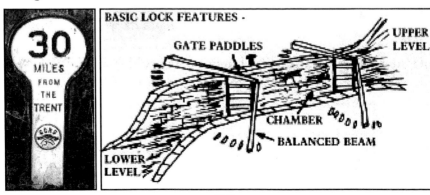

OTHER CANAL WALK GUIDES
by John N. Merrill

VOL ONE - DERBYSHIRE AND NOTTINGHAMSHIRE - More than 30 walks, both short and long, on the Erewash, Derby, Trent & Mersey, Nottingham, Beeston and Nutbrook canals. The guide is not just a walk guide but a historical guide to what can be seen today and a photographic essay to canals in the area. 128 pages 60 photographs 32 maps
ISBN 1-903627-53 -2 £12.95 - wire bound **new enlarged edition**

VOL TWO - CHESHIRE AND STAFFORDSHIRE - Details more than 40 circular walks on the Peak Forest, Macclesfield Caldon and Trent & Mersey canals. Like Vol. 1, a major reference source to canal walking on the western side of the Pennines. All are circular and include both long and short walks with numerous pubs along the way. 88 pages 61 photographs 27 maps ISBN 0 907496 38 5 Wire bound. £9.95

VOL THREE—STAFFORDSHIRE - 36 short circular walks on the Trent & Mersey, Coventry, Staffordshire & Worcestershire Canals within the boundary of Staffordshire, between Stoke on Trent and Burton Upon Trent. This book links together Vol. 1 & 2 of the series. 84 pages 60 photographs 30 maps ISBN 0 907496 62 8 Wire bound £9.95

VOL FOUR—THE CHESHIRE RING - Walk guide with history notes to the 97 mile walk around the ring on the Macclesfield, Peak Forest, Ashton, Rochdale, Bridgewater, and Trent & Mersey Canals. Comprehensive amenities guide to enable you to walk it in stages or as a weeks walk. 80 pages 38 colour photographs 15 maps ISBN 1-903627-39-7 £9.95 wire bound.
New edition

VOL FIVE—THE GRANTHAM CANAL More than fifteen walks on the Grantham Canal, from the River Trent to Grantham. Unspoilt walking in the Vale of Belvoir. 96 pages 40 colour photographs 16 maps
ISBN 1-903627-56-7 £11.95 **NEW**

WALKING THE TRENT & MERSEY CANAL - Walk guide to the whole length of the canal end-to-end from Preston Brook to Shardlow and Derwent Mouth. 93 miles of some of the finest canal walking in Britain. Amenities guide and walk described in stages. 64 pages 35 photographs 18 maps ISBN 1 874754 19 5.   £9.95

WALKING THE LLANGOLLEN CANAL A complete end to end walk from Nantwich to Llangollen -50 miles, along the canl. The scenery is oustanding and the canal features are unsurpassed. ISBN 1 84173 017 3 56 pages. 25 photographs. 10 maps. £8.95

WALKING THE DERBY CANAL RING - A magnificent 28 mile walk from the centre of Derby, following the line of the Derby Canal to the Trent & Mersey Canal and onto the River Trent and Erewash Canal. You return to Derby along the line of the Sandiacre section of the Derby Canal. ISBN 1874754 28 4. 32 pages. 5 maps. 10 photographs. £6.95

THE SALT & SAILS TRAIL by David Burkhill Howarth. - A magnificent 20 mile walk from Weston Point to Winsford along the Weaver Navigation in Cheshire, with very detailed history notes. ISBN 1 874754 58 6. 44 pages. 7 maps. 10 photographs. £5.95
.

SHORT CIRCULAR WALKS IN THE CHESTERFIELD CANAL More than fifteen walks on the Chesterfield Canall, from Chesterfield via Worksop to the River Trent at West Stockwith. Unspoilt walking Derbyshire & Nottinghamshire. 112 pages 45 photographs 16 maps ISBN 1-903627-56-7 £10.95. Colour edition £14.95. Wire bound.

SHORT CIRCULAR WALKS ON THE CROMFORD CANAL Ten walks on the Cromford Canal, from Cromford to the Great Northern Basin at Langley.. Unspoilt walking, tracing the abandoned canal and Pinxton Arm. 96 pages 45 photographs 16 maps ISBN 1-903627-54-0 £8.95. Colour edition £10.95 Wire bound.

SHORT CIRCULAR WALKS ON THE RIVER LEE NAVIGATION - (London to Hertford) - Northern Volume.
60 pages, 23 photographs, 10 detailed maps and walks - walks between Ponders End Lock and Hertford. History notes. ISBN 1-903627-68-0 £7.95 **NEW**

SHORT CIRCULAR WALKS ON THE RIVER STORT NAVIGATION
Despite only being 13 1/2 miles long from the River Lee Navigation, near Broxbourne to Bishop's Stortford, the navigation is a gem and full of history. Eight circular walks explore its full length and one explores it end to end. The guide is not just a walk one, but a history of the canal and surrounding villages and a photographic essay.
92 pages, 68 colour photographs, 12 maps. Wire bound.
ISBN 1-903627-73-7 £10.95 **NEW**

SHORT CIRCULAR WALKS ON THE RIVER LEE NAVIGATION - (London to Hertford) - Southern Volume.
68 pages, 33 photographs, 12 detailed maps and walks - walks between Limehouse Basin/River Thames and Enfield Lock. Includes Bow Creek River and City Mill Rivers. Includes 28 mile end to end walk - Limehouse Basin to Hertford.
Considerable History notes. ISBN 1-903627-74-5 £7.95 **NEW**

WALKING THE CANALS OF LONDON
End to End walks and circular walks on the Regent's Canal and Union Canal and the Paddington Branch, and exploraton of the Isle of Dogs and River Thames. Plus a London Canal Loop walk of 52 miles.
104 pages. 96 colour photographs. 18 maps. Wire Bound.
ISBN 978-0-9553691-2-4 £10.95 NEW

WALKING THE RIVER LEE NAVIGATION - 20 walks.
Both the South and North volumes in one book, plus additional walks around the 2012 Olympic Park area. ISBN 978-09553691-8-6 108 pages. Wire bound. £9.95 NEW

SHORT CIRCULAR WALKS IN THE COLNE VALLEY (Grand Union Canal) 8 walks - 3 to 11 miles long - that full eplore the area between Rickmansworth and Slough. One 20 mile walk - Rickmansworth to the River Thames.
72 pages. 12 maps. 40 photographs. ISBN 978-0-9560649-5-0 £7.95 NEW

WALKING THE CHELMER AND BLACKWATER NAVIGATION - 16 MILES - From Maldon to Chelmsford, Essex, beside this stunning and unspoilt waterway. NEW 2011

OTHER JOHN MERRILL WALK BOOKS

CIRCULAR WALK GUIDES -
SHORT CIRCULAR WALKS IN THE PEAK DISTRICT - VOL. 1,2, 3 AND 9
CIRCULAR WALKS IN WESTERN PEAKLAND
SHORT CIRCULAR WALKS IN THE STAFFORDSHIRE MOORLANDS
SHORT CIRCULAR WALKS - TOWNS & VILLAGES OF THE PEAK DISTRICT
SHORT CIRCULAR WALKS AROUND MATLOCK
SHORT CIRCULAR WALKS IN "PEAK PRACTICE COUNTRY."
SHORT CIRCULAR WALKS IN THE DUKERIES
SHORT CIRCULAR WALKS IN SOUTH YORKSHIRE
SHORT CIRCULAR WALKS IN SOUTH DERBYSHIRE
SHORT CIRCULAR WALKS AROUND BUXTON
SHORT CIRCULAR WALKS AROUND WIRKSWORTH
SHORT CIRCULAR WALKS IN THE HOPE VALLEY
40 SHORT CIRCULAR WALKS IN THE PEAK DISTRICT
CIRCULAR WALKS ON KINDER & BLEAKLOW
SHORT CIRCULAR WALKS IN SOUTH NOTTINGHAMSHIRE
SHORT CIRCULAR WALKS IN CHESHIRE
SHORT CIRCULAR WALKS IN WEST YORKSHIRE
WHITE PEAK DISTRICT AIRCRAFT WRECKS
CIRCULAR WALKS IN THE DERBYSHIRE DALES
SHORT CIRCULAR WALKS FROM BAKEWELL
SHORT CIRCULAR WALKS IN LATHKILL DALE
CIRCULAR WALKS IN THE WHITE PEAK
SHORT CIRCULAR WALKS IN EAST DEVON
SHORT CIRCULAR WALKS AROUND HARROGATE
SHORT CIRCULAR WALKS IN CHARNWOOD FOREST
SHORT CIRCULAR WALKS AROUND CHESTERFIELD
SHORT CIRCULAR WALKS IN THE YORKS DALES - Vol 1 - SOUTHERN AREA.
SHORT CIRCULAR WALKS IN THE AMBER VALLEY (DERBYSHIRE)
SHORT CIRCULAR WALKS IN THE LAKE DISTRICT
SHORT CIRCULAR WALKS IN THE NORTH YORKSHIRE MOORS
SHORT CIRCULAR WALKS IN EAST STAFFORDSHIRE
LONG CIRCULAR WALKS IN THE PEAK DISTRICT - VOL.1, 2 , 3, 4 AND 5.
DARK PEAK AIRCRAFT WRECK WALKS
LONG CIRCULAR WALKS IN THE STAFFORDSHIRE MOORLANDS
LONG CIRCULAR WALKS IN CHESHIRE
WALKING THE TISSINGTON TRAIL
WALKING THE HIGH PEAK TRAIL
WALKING THE MONSAL TRAIL & SETT VALLEY TRAILS
PEAK DISTRICT WALKING - TEN "TEN MILER'S" - Vol ONE AND TWO
CLIMB THE PEAKS OF THE PEAK DISTRICT
PEAK DISTRICT WALK A MONTH Vols ONE,TWO, THREE, FOUR, FIVE & SIX
TRAIN TO WALK Vol. ONE - THE HOPE VALLEY LINE
DERBYSHIRE LOST VILLAGE WALKS -Vol ONE AND TWO.
CIRCULAR WALKS IN DOVEDALE AND THE MANIFOLD VALLEY
CIRCULAR WALKS AROUND GLOSSOP
WALKING THE LONGDENDALE TRAIL
WALKING THE UPPER DON TRAIL
SHORT CIRCULAR WALKS IN CANNOCK CHASE
CIRCULAR WALKS IN THE DERWENT VALLEY
WALKING THE TRAILS OF NORTH-EAST DERBYSHIRE
WALKING THE PENNINE BRIDLEWAY & CIRCULAR WALKS
SHORT CIRCULAR WALKS ON THE NEW RIVER & SOUTH-EAST HERTFORDSHIRE
SHORT CIRCULAR WALKS IN EPPING FOREST
WALKING THE STREETS OF LONDON
LONG CIRCULAR WALKS IN EASTERN HERTFORDSHIRE
LONG CIRCULAR WALKS IN WESTERN HERTFORDSHIRE
WALKS IN THE LONDON BOROUGH OF ENFIELD
WALKS IN THE LONDON BOROUGH OF BARNET
WALKS IN THE LONDON BOROUGH OF HARINGEY
WALK IN THE LONDON BOROUGH OF WALTHAM FOREST
SHORT CIRCULAR WALKS AROUND HERTFORD
THE BIG WALKS OF LONDON
SHORT CIRCULAR WALKS AROUND BISHOP'S STORTFORD
SHORT CIRCULAR WALKS AROUND EPPING DISTRICT
CIRCULAR WALKS IN THE BOROUGH OF BROXBOURNE
LONDON INTERFAITH WALKS - Vol 1 AND VOL. 2
LONG CIRCULAR WALKS IN THE NORTH CHILTERNS
SHORT CIRCULAR WALKS IN EASTERN HERTFORDSHIRE
WORCESTERSHIRE VILLAGE WALKS BY DES WRIGHT
WARWICKSHIRE VILLAGE WALKS BY DES WRIGHT

For a free complete catalogue of John Merrill walk Guides send a SAE to The John Merrill Foundation

CANAL WALKS -
VOL 1 - DERBYSHIRE & NOTTINGHAMSHIRE
VOL 2 - CHESHIRE & STAFFORDSHIRE
VOL 3 - STAFFORDSHIRE
VOL 4 - THE CHESHIRE RING
VOL 5 - THE GRANTHAM CANAL
VOL 6 - SOUTH YORKSHIRE
VOL 7 - THE TRENT & MERSEY CANAL
VOL 8 - WALKING THE DERBY CANAL RING
VOL 9 - WALKING THE LLANGOLLEN CANAL
VOL 10 - CIRCULAR WALKS ON THE CHESTERFIELD CANAL
VOL 11 - CIRCULAR WALKS ON THE CROMFORD CANAL
VOL.13 - SHORT CIRCULAR WALKS ON THE RIVER LEE NAVIGATION -Vol. 1 - NORTH
VOL. 14 - SHORT CIRCULAR WALKS ON THE RIVER STORT NAVIGATION
VOL.15 - SHORT CIRCULAR WALKS ON THE RIVER LEE NAVIGATION - Vol. 2 - SOUTH
VOL. 16 - WALKING THE CANALS OF LONDON
VOL 17 - WALKING THE RIVER LEE NAVIGATION
VOL. 20 - SHORT CIRCULAR WALKS IN THE COLNE VALLEY
Vol 21 - THE BLACKWATER & CHELMER NAVIGATION - END TO END.

Visit our website -
www.johnmerrillwalkguides.com

JOHN MERRILL DAY CHALLENGE WALKS -
WHITE PEAK CHALLENGE WALK
THE HAPPY HIKER - WHITE PEAK - CHALLENGE WALK No.2
DARK PEAK CHALLENGE WALK
PEAK DISTRICT END TO END WALKS
STAFFORDSHIRE MOORLANDS CHALLENGE WALK
THE LITTLE JOHN CHALLENGE WALK
YORKSHIRE DALES CHALLENGE WALK

97

NORTH YORKSHIRE MOORS CHALLENGE WALK
LAKELAND CHALLENGE WALK
THE RUTLAND WATER CHALLENGE WALK
MALVERN HILLS CHALLENGE WALK
THE SALTER'S WAY
THE SNOWDON CHALLENGE
CHARNWOOD FOREST CHALLENGE WALK
THREE COUNTIES CHALLENGE WALK (PEAK DISTRICT).
CAL-DER-WENT WALK BY GEOFFREY CARR,
THE QUANTOCK WAY
BELVOIR WITCHES CHALLENGE WALK
THE CARNEDDAU CHALLENGE WALK
THE SWEET PEA CHALLENGE WALK
THE LINCOLNSHIRE WOLDS - BLACK DEATH - CHALLENGE WALK
JENNIFER'S CHALLENGE WALK
THE EPPING FOREST CHALLENGE WALK
THE THREE BOROUGH CHALLENGE WALK - NORTH LONDON

INSTRUCTION & RECORD -
HIKE TO BE FIT.....STROLLING WITH JOHN
THE JOHN MERRILL WALK RECORD BOOK
HIKE THE WORLD - JOHN MERRILL'S GUIDE TO WALKING & BACKPACKING.

MULTIPLE DAY WALKS -
THE RIVERS'S WAY
PEAK DISTRICT: HIGH LEVEL ROUTE
PEAK DISTRICT MARATHONS
THE LIMEY WAY
THE PEAKLAND WAY
COMPO'S WAY BY ALAN HILEY
THE BRIGHTON WAY

THE PILGRIM WALKS SERIES -
THE WALSINGHAM WAY - ELY TO WALSINGHAM - 72 MILES
THE WALSINGHAM WAY - KINGS LYNN TO WALSINGHAM - 35 MILES
TURN LEFT AT GRANJA DE LA MORERUELA - 700 MILES
NORTH TO SANTIAGO DE COMPOSTELA, VIA FATIMA - 650 MILES
ST. OLAV'S WAY - OSLO TO TRONDHEIM - 400 MILES
ST. WINEFRIDE'S WAY - ST. ASAPH TO HOLYWELL
ST. ALBANS WAY - WALTHAM ABBEY TO ST. ALBANS - 26 MILES
ST. KENELM TRAIL BY JOHN PRICE - CLENT HILLS TO WINCHCOMBE - 60 MILES
DERBYSHIRE PILGRIMAGES
LONDON TO CANTERBURY- 75 MILES
LONDON TO ST. ALBANS - 36 MILES
LONDON TO WALSINGHAM - 194 MILES
FOLKESTONE, HYTHE TO CANTERBURY - 25 MILES
THE JOHN SCHORNE PEREGRINATIONS - 27 MILES BY M. MOONEY
ST CEDD'S PILGRIMAGE WALK - 24 MILES
ST BIRINIUS PILGRIMAGE WALK - 26 MILES
OUR LADY OF ULTING PILGRIMAGE WALK - 16 MILES
OUR LADY OF CAVERSHAM PILGRIMAGE WALK - 38 MILES
THE MANDEVILLE MONKS WAY - 32 MILES
THE ESSEX PRIORIES WAY - 20 MILES
WALKING THE CAMMINO DI ASSISI - 320 KM.
A FUNERAL CELEBRANT'S DIARY

COAST WALKS & NATIONAL TRAILS -
ISLE OF WIGHT COAST PATH
PEMBROKESHIRE COAST PATH
THE CLEVELAND WAY
WALKING ANGELSEY'S COASTLINE.
WALKING THE COASTLINE OF THE CHANNEL ISLANDS
THE ISLE OF MAN COASTAL PATH - "THE WAY OF THE GULL."
A WALK AROUND HAYLING ISLAND
A WALK AROUND THE ISLE OF SHEPPEY
A WALK AROUND THE ISLE OF JERSEY
WALKING AROUND THE ISLANDS OF ESSEX

DERBYSHIRE & PEAK DISTRICT HISTORICAL GUIDES -
A TO Z GUIDE OF THE PEAK DISTRICT
DERBYSHIRE INNS - AN A TO Z GUIDE
HALLS AND CASTLES OF THE PEAK DISTRICT & DERBYSHIRE
TOURING THE PEAK DISTRICT & DERBYSHIRE BY CAR
DERBYSHIRE FOLKLORE
PUNISHMENT IN DERBYSHIRE
CUSTOMS OF THE PEAK DISTRICT & DERBYSHIRE
WINSTER - A SOUVENIR GUIDE
ARKWRIGHT OF CROMFORD
LEGENDS OF DERBYSHIRE
DERBYSHIRE FACTS & RECORDS
TALES FROM THE MINES BY GEOFFREY CARR
PEAK DISTRICT PLACE NAMES BY MARTIN SPRAY
DERBYSHIRE THROUGH THE AGES - VOL 1 -DERBYSHIRE IN PREHISTORIC TIMES
SIR JOSEPH PAXTON
FLORENCE NIGHTINGALE
JOHN SMEDLEY
BONNIE PRINCE CHARLIE & 20 MILE WALK.
THE STORY OF THE EARLS AND DUKES OF DEVONSHIRE

JOHN MERRILL'S MAJOR WALKS -
TURN RIGHT AT LAND'S END
WITH MUSTARD ON MY BACK
TURN RIGHT AT DEATH VALLEY
EMERALD COAST WALK
I CHOSE TO WALK - WHY I WALK ETC.
A WALK IN OHIO - 1,310 MILES AROUND THE BUCKEYE TRAIL.
I AM GUIDED - THE STORY OF JOHN'S LIFE.

SKETCH BOOKS -
SKETCHES OF THE PEAK DISTRICT

COLOUR BOOK:-
THE PEAK DISTRICT.......SOMETHING TO REMEMBER HER BY.

OVERSEAS GUIDES -
HIKING IN NEW MEXICO - VOL I - THE SANDIA AND MANZANO MOUNTAINS.
VOL 2 - HIKING "BILLY THE KID" COUNTRY. VOL 4 - N.W. AREA - " HIKING INDIAN COUNTRY."
"WALKING IN DRACULA COUNTRY" - ROMANIA.
WALKING THE TRAILS OF THE HONG KONG ISLANDS.

VISITOR GUIDES - MATLOCK . BAKEWELL. ASHBOURNE.

COMPANION CANAL GUIDES -

THE DERBYSHIRE CANAL WALKS SERIES - Vol Two

SHORT CIRCULAR WALKS ON THE CROMFORD CANAL

The Brixton child

by John N. Merrill

Eleven circular walks on the Cromford Canal,
berween Cromford and Langley Mill.

CANAL WALKS - Vol. One

Short Circular walks on the Canals of

Derbyshire and Nottinghamshire

by John N. Merrill

More than twenty walks on the Nottingham, Beeston, Erewash, and Trent & Mersey Canals and the River Trent.

WALKING THE
DERBY CANAL RING

by John N. Merrill

Walk the Derby Ring - 28 miles - following the line of the Derby
Canal and the Trent & Mersey and Erewash Canals. The
successful can obtain a special embroidered badge and signed
certificate.

THE CANAL WALKS SERIES

Walking the Trent & Mersey Canal

by John N. Merrill

Walk the Trent & Mersey Canal End to End - a magnificent level
100 mile walk from Runcorn, Cheshire to Shardlow, Derbyshire.
The successful can obtain a special badge and signed certificate.

SHORT CIRCULAR WALKS
on the
CHESTERFIELD CANAL

Twenty walks exploring the full length of this unique canal from Chesterfield to West Stockwith and the River Trent.

The Belvoir Witches Challenge Walk is a magnificent walk around the Vale of Belvoir, where in the 17th. century three witches resided. The walk is a challenge to do in a day - 25 miles, but can be done over a weekend, passing through exceptional countryside - the Grantham Canal, picturesque villages, woodland and Belvoir Castle. A badge and certificate are available for the successful. The walk starts and ends at Bottesford.

Book available from The John Merrill Foundation.

The Art of walking the John Merrill Way.

1. Always set off in the clothes you plan to wear all day, given the weather conditions. Only on sudden changes in the weather will I stop and put on a waterproof or warmer clothing.

2. Set off at a steady comfortable pace, which you can maintain all day. You should end the walk as fresh as when you started.

3. Maintain your pace and don't stop. Stopping for any period of time disrupts your rythmn and takes upwards of a mile (20 mins) to settle back down into the flow/ease of movement.

4. Switch your phone off. Listen and enjoy the countryside - the smell of the flowers, bird song, the rustle of leaves and the tinkling stream, and observe the wildlife.

5. Ignore the mileage and ascents - don't tick the miles or hills, just concentrate on what the walk's goal is. To think otherwise slows you down and makes the walk a struggle rather than a joy. In a similar vein, when ascending just keep a steady pace and keep going. To stop is to disrupt the flow and make the ascent interminable.

6. Whist a walk is a challenge to complete, it is not just exercise. You should enjoy the world around you, the flowers, birds, wildlife and nature and look at and explore the historical buildings and churches that you pass. Industrial complex's have their own beauty. All are part of life's rich tapestry.

7. Remember that for every mile you walk, you extend your life by 21 minutes.

8. A journey of a 1,000 miles begins with a single step and a mile requires 2,000 strides.

"The expert traveller leaves no footprints" Lao Tzu.

THE JOHN MERRILL FOUNDATION LONG DISTANCE WALKING CHARTER FOR THE UK.

1. All path signs to be made of wood and clearly state the right of way designation and destination, with correct mileage/kilometers. Individually designed, logo or symbols is to be encouraged. Variety and individuality is essential.

2. Wooden stiles are preferred to kissing gates. Kissing gates have a fatal flaw - many are not wide enough yo allow a backpacker with his pack to get in and out of without removing the pack. For half the year the central area is wet and muddy. The metal bar stiles with a wide base and narrow neck at thew top should be abolished; they are not suitable for backpackers - all have to take the rucksacks off to get through.
SOS - *Save our stiles* - part of our heritage.

3. All long distance routes to clearly state the start and end of the route on the ground, with an overall map showing the route at each end. Registration boxes at either end for signing in and out.

4. All long distance routes should provide regular places for wild camping. No ammenities required just a place to pitch a tent.

5. All temporary path closures should be notified from the nearest road and not at the start of a particular path - this results in having to walk back. The diversion or temporay alternative route should be clearly well signed.

6. Every walker should be trained to read a map, use a compass and calculate a gride reference. The dependence of modern technology is to be encouraged - but learn the basic skills.

7. All long distance walkers should wear well broken in and good fitting boots, wkith two pairs of socks, and carry the minumum basics in a suitable padded and framed rucksack.

8. All footpaths & rights of way's should be be regularly cleared of brambles, nettles, blow downs, and overhanging branches to allow a walker to pass through comfortably. Paths should be natural earth, not gravel, tarmac or rock slab.

9. Take your rubbish home - pack it in, pack it out.

10. Take only pictures.

11. Admire the flowers but do not pick them.

12. Say "hello" to all walkers that you pass.

13. Leave your headphones, music centre at home so you can enjoy the sounds of nature. Switch your phone off and only use in an emergency.

May the sun bring you new energy by day,
May the moon softly restore you by night,
May the rain wash away your worries,
May the breeze blow new strength into your being,
May you walk gently through the world and
Know it's beauty all the days of your life.

Apache blessing.

Look at the tees,
Look at the birds,
Look at the clouds,
Look at the stars ....
And if you have eyes
you will be able to see
that the whole of
existence is joyful.

Osho

THE JOHN MERRILL MINISTRY
- a universal monk - embracing & honouring
all faiths & none.

John has been following his own spiritual path all his life, and is guided. He was brought up as a Christian and confirmed at the age of 13. He then went to a Quaker Boarding School for five years and developed his love for the countryside and walking. He became fascinated with Tibet and whilst retaining his Christian roots, became immersed in Buddhism. For four years he studied at the Tara Buddhist Centre in Derbyshire. He progressed into Daoism and currently attends the Chinese Buddhist Temple (Pure Land Tradition) in London. With his thirst for knowledge and discovery he paid attention to other faiths and appreciated their values. Late in life he decided it was time to reveal his spiritual beliefs and practices and discovered the Interfaith Seminary.

'When the pupil is ready, the teacher will appear'. (Buddhist saying).

Here for two years he learnt in more depth the whole spectrum of faiths , including Jainism, Paganism, Mother Earth, Buddhism, Hinduism, Islam, Judaism, Sikhism, Celtic Worship and Shamanism. This is an ongoing exploration without end. He embraces all faiths, for all have a beauty of their own. All paths/faiths lead to one goal/truth. On July 17th. 2010 he was Ordained as a Multi-faith Minister.

'May you go in peace, with joy in your heart
and may the divine be always at your side.'

Using his knowledge and experience he combines many faiths into a simple, caring and devoted services, individually made for each specific occasion, with dignity and honour.
He conducts special Ceremonies -

Popular Funeral Celebrant and member of the Natural Death Society.

* Funerals * Memorial Services * Sermons * Weddings   *Civil Partnerships * Baby Blessings & Naming
* Rites of Passage * Healing Ceremonies * Pilgimages * Inspirational Talks
Qigong Teacher.   Reiki Prationer.

For further information Contact John on -
Tel/Fax: 01992 - 762776   Mobile. 07910 889429
Email - buddhaonfoot@mail.com
Ministry site -www.thejohnmerrillministry.co.uk
All Faiths church - www.londoninterfaithchurch.co.uk

Revd. John N. Merrill, HonMUni